1993

We hope this offers you
insight and inspiration
for your upcoming trip!

Love, Rodger & Elaine

Walkers
TRADITIONS OF SCOTLAND

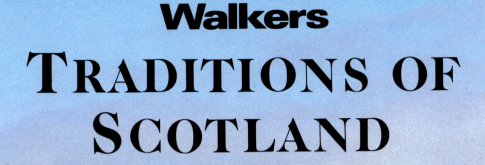

Walkers
TRADITIONS OF SCOTLAND

Gilbert Summers

With a foreword by Mary, Countess of Strathmore and Kinghorne

MARTIN BOOKS

Acknowledgements

The publishers would like to thank the following individuals and organisations, to whom copyright in the photographs mentioned below belongs, for the loan of transparencies used in this book:

Donald Addison/Paper Sky: page 119; Alba Pictures: page 135; Aviemore Photographic: pages 67, 74, 114–15; BTA/ETB/SI: pages 19, 26–7, 147; Charles Tait Photographic: page 131; Douglas Corrance: pages 10–11; Historic Scotland: page 98; Loch Lomond, Stirling and Trossachs Tourist Board: page 22; National Gallery of Scotland: page 94; Scottish National Portrait Gallery: pages 31, 34, 38, 86, 89; Scottish Tourist Board: page 127; STB Still Moving Picture Company: front cover; Gilbert Summers: pages 2–3, 14, 43, 46, 82–3, 90, 139, 154; Walkers Shortbread Ltd: pages 50, 78 and back cover; Hugh Webster/The Scottish Highland Photolibrary: pages 54–5, 71, 142; Robin Williams/Vanellus: page 58.

The picture on page 62 is reproduced by gracious permission of Her Majesty the Queen.

MARTIN BOOKS

Published by Martin Books
Simon & Schuster Consumer Group
Fitzwilliam House
32 Trumpington Street
Cambridge CB2 1QY

in association with
Walkers Shortbread Ltd
Aberlour-on-Spey
Scotland AB3 9PB

First published 1991
© Woodhead-Faulkner (Publishers) Ltd

ISBN 0 85941 708 5

Design: Clare Byatt
Photography on pages 103, 110: Laurie Evans
Photography on page 106: Steve Lee
Illustrations: Harriet Dell/Graham Cameron Illustration

Typesetting: Ace Filmsetting Ltd, Frome, Somerset
Printed and bound by Grafedit S. P. A. Bergamo, Italy

Picture on previous page: Fraserburgh harbour

Contents

T HE S COTS H ERITAGE

Living traditions

Scotland is as modern and forward-looking as anywhere else. Yet it has a curious habit of harking back to its traditions and its past. Probably any writer who produces material on Scotland encounters this paradox. Certainly, it has always fascinated me. I have been lucky enough to have been given the opportunity to write about my home country and to look at some of the points where past and present meet – from Hallowe'en to Highland Games. Walkers Shortbread, who are a good example of this mingling of tradition with modernity, hope it will answer some of the questions about Scotland that they are often asked. I

Decorative interlacing and bird heads are examples of a Celtic art form found, among other places, on jewellery, weapons and grave goods, stonework (especially carved crosses) and manuscript illustration. This example, from The Book of Kells, *recalls the Irish connection in Scotland's story: this great gospel book dating from around the eighth century may have been made in Iona, cradle of Scottish Christianity, or in Kells in Ireland.*

hope so too, but also hope it will send the reader off to find out more and to explore beyond the tartan curtain.

Scotland is a small country, its history bound up for centuries with its larger and more powerful neighbour, England. It surrendered its own nationhood in 1707, yet has never forgotten it. Highland people were scattered abroad both by strife and by the harshness of life in an unforgiving landscape, yet the curious magic of Scotland still casts a spell on each succeeding generation – on Scots at home and abroad, and on those who aspire to be adopted by this unyielding rocky land reaching out in the cold northern seas. Scotland hangs on to 'Scottishness' in voice, attitude, even dress and food, in spite of the levelling effects of the modern media, generations of schoolmasters, and the tempting road which leads to London, England, and beyond.

An undercurrent of old beliefs and values, as well as living links with traditional ways of thinking, can be found in many parts of Scotland. Even the fisherman in his modern vessel, fully-equipped with electronic catching aids, is only two or three generations apart from the men of the open-decked boats, with only sail and muscle power to help them, whose daily lives were bound up with superstition and sea-lore.

Scotland's personality is also retained in the sheer vitality of its traditional images. Bagpipes and Highland dress, and all the paraphernalia of a modern clan gathering, have come far from the days when a cattle-droving

Highlander depended on his long plaid for survival on a frosty night on the open hillside, or when chieftains used tests of strength to select their most powerful warriors. Yet, even when modified and packaged for the benefit of visitors, today's Highland Games, with their unique recipe of skill and strength as well as musical events, are recognisable descendants of the ancient customs.

To the outsider, Scotland means clans and tartans. But even this seemingly quintessential Scottish tradition has had a curious history. In 1746, the traditional garb of the Highlander was banned by order of a government in Westminster fearful of northern rebellions. Less than a century later, it was being worn by the highest in the land as an item of fashion and has since become the very symbol of Scotland itself, Highland or Lowland.

A sense of Scottish identity starts at the Border, not the Highland line, and this is proved by the strength of feeling and vigour of the annual gatherings in Border towns. Scotland's struggle for independence and its desire to play a part in wider European affairs often brought it into conflict with England. And when matters were settled by military force – as they usually were – it was the Border towns which inevitably suffered most. There, the need to protect the bounds, to repel raiding parties or to be prepared to mount and take up arms was the strongest. This very real threat has evolved into a tradition of mounted gatherings and rideouts known as Common Ridings, now quite peaceful, which recall the stirring events of the past.

Not all have been continuous: the celebration at the town of Galashiels, called the Braw Lads Gathering, was founded as recently as 1930, though it incorporates very old local legends and traditions. However, the little town of Selkirk claims a Common Riding that is at least 400 years old – a festival chiefly known for its intention of keeping the memory of the Battle of Flodden alive. This battle in 1513 was one of the worst defeats at the hands of the English. All of the Border communities lost men. Tradition relates that 80 went to Flodden from Selkirk but only one returned, though he was bearing a captured English flag. An element in today's celebrations at Selkirk is the 'casting of the colours', an event which recalls this incident.

Language is an important element in the Scottish psyche: not just Gaelic, the ancient language of the clans, but Lowland Scots, a surviving dialect rich in borrowings from Scandinavian, French and Dutch. After generations of trying to imitate the dialect of England's Thames Valley, commonly known as 'standard English', more and more Scots are beginning to appreciate the heritage of their own tongue as a vital part of their sense of 'Scottishness'. Historical links with France in particular are enshrined in the Scots tongue and can still be heard today, with a variety of traditional culinary terms recalling the French influence in the Scots kitchen, for example.

Scots (and their descendants overseas) have a strong tradition of a yearning for the beauties of the Scottish landscape. 'The Banks of Loch Lomond' is just one of the songs that celebrate the countryside with a touch of melancholy: the exile's nostalgia for 'home' – even when he

Botanical queries are sometimes raised as to which species of thistle is the Scottish one. Tradition relates how an encampment of Scots in ancient times was alerted to a raiding party of Danes when one of the raiders stepped barefoot on a thistle in the darkness and yelled in pain! The thistle became a symbol of Scotland thereafter.

or she has never lived there. To live amongst the bens and glens seems to have been an aspiration of a whole generation of Scottish song-writers of the 'Grannie's Heilan Hame' variety. Yet the 'traditional' life in Scotland, particularly in the Highlands, must always have been hard, even though the Gaelic oral tradition celebrated the routines of work, the passing of the seasons and the joys of love and companionship in song. It was this lifestyle that was swept aside by the Highland Clearances to leave the empty land so desired by the visitor today as an antidote to city stress.

The tumbled walls and scattered stone of these abandoned settlements can still be seen in the Highlands. Stray into a high corrie (a glacier-cut mountain valley) and you are likely to stumble across the ruins of sheilings. These were the traditional summer shelters used by the clan-folk while looking after their cattle, taken alpine-style to high summer grazings. Now this way of life has vanished and these old traditions are replaced by others – by a rapidly growing tradition which sees the Highlands as a place of recreation, for example. This perhaps had its origins in the growth of exclusive and strictly private sporting estates bought by southern industrialists in the nineteenth century. Today, with an ever increasing army of outdoor enthusiasts, and as many as 279 peaks over 914 m (3,000 ft), it might be said that hillwalking is one of the most rapidly growing traditional activities in the Highlands.

Living traditions can be noted in events and gatherings of various kinds all over Scotland, although the customs and habits themselves may have evolved and changed with the passage of time. Some, like the summer sheilings, died off or disappeared almost literally into the Highland landscape. Other aspects of the Scots' heritage are still very much in evidence, some even hang in the breeze! One of the pleasures of Scotland is the range of smells to be savoured. You can enjoy the warm and yeasty smell of the city brewery or the dusty air of a mill producing oatmeal for porridge.

The properties of rowan wood were valued not just for their practical use but for their ability to guard the household against witches and evil spells. Thus, in olden times, the supporting crossbeam on the chimney would often have been made from this 'lucky' wood, while a guardian rowan tree would be planted just outside the door.

Around the fishing ports of the north-east, the range of odours from the fish processing plants is certainly pungent. Travel up to Speyside and through the woodlands comes that most characteristic steamy scent of a distillery, sometimes sharp, sometimes sweet. In Aberlour a particularly appetising aroma awaits. Walkers, the old established local baker, send their shortbread all over the world from this quiet little community. A fresh-made, rich and buttery smell greets the visitor, triggering nostalgia for traditional home-baking of long ago.

At such moments, old practices and modern methods are one. Perhaps that is part of Scotland's appeal – an acknowledgement of the past, and an intention of keeping the best from its heritage, yet an ability to face the future with a strong identity.

FOREWORD

I am very honoured indeed to have been asked to write the fore-word to this lovely book, *Traditions of Scotland*.

Living as I have for many years at Glamis Castle makes one especially aware of Scotland's history and traditions.

Scotland has a national identity recognised throughout the world. Who has not heard of Robert Burns, haggis, kilts, the Loch Ness monster and Scotch whisky? Who is not familiar with the haunting melodies of 'The Skye Boat Song' and the wistful 'Will Ye No' Come Back Again'? More importantly than all these, I feel Scotland is recognised for the quality of its people, and throughout the world you will find Scottish people doing important jobs, and appreciated for their integrity and hard working qualities.

I also like to think that we are known as a hospitable people who make visitors who come to see our beautiful country feel welcome and at home. It has given me great pleasure for many years to welcome thousands of visitors from all over the world who come to see my historic home.

Walkers Shortbread has for many years been one of our country's foremost ambassadors. So many people have first been introduced to Scotland through Walkers' traditional bakery products and the historical scenes represented on their packaging. It is particularly appropriate, therefore, that they should be the sponsors of this beautiful book which encapsulates in its pages the spirit of Scotland, its history, traditions, personalities and folklore.

I very much hope that you will enjoy reading *Traditions of Scotland* and that its beautiful illustrations and fascinating accounts of history and traditions inspire you to visit Scotland to discover for yourself the curious magic of our very varied and interesting small country.

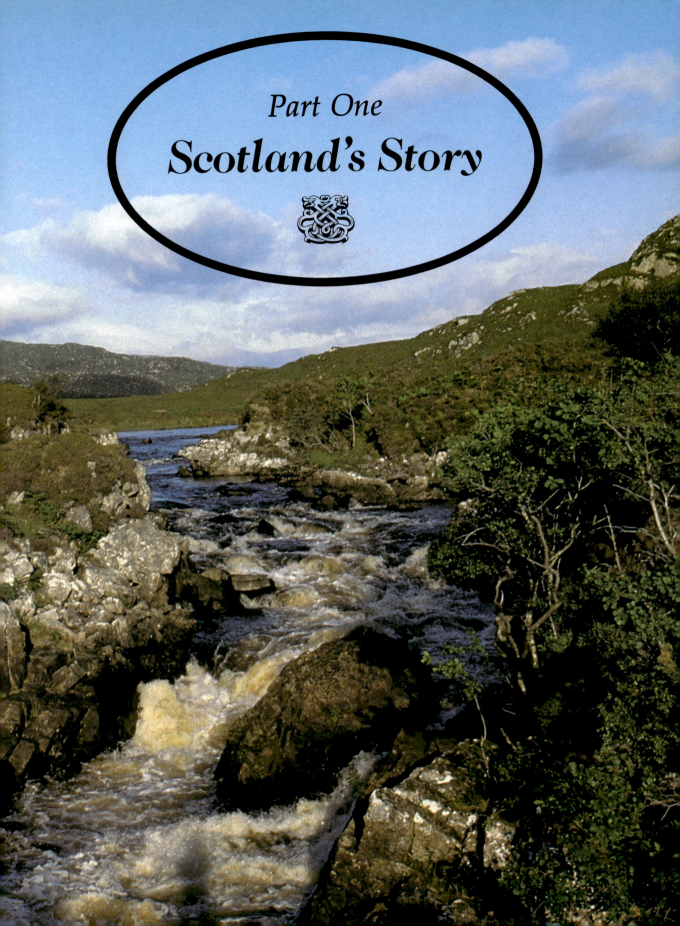

Part One
Scotland's Story

 ONE

EARLY PEOPLE:

The Emergence of Scotland

The first shadowy wanderers seem to have discovered Scotland some time after the ending of the last Ice Age, about 8,000 years ago. Hunter-gatherers for survival, they probed along the shores at the edge of dark forests, fearsome and unknown. The middens – the shell and fishbone dumps – of these early folk have survived to provide clues for the archaeologist, but life in later Stone-Age Scotland is more palpable from some of the prehistoric sites of the Northern Isles.

At the Knap of Howar on Papa Westray in Orkney, the visitor can see a neolithic (new Stone Age) farmstead, still complete to the top of the wall height. This is often claimed to be the oldest house in Europe, dated around 3000 BC. Archaeologists have deduced from it that, far from being simply primitive hunters, its builders cultivated wheat and barley and reared cattle and sheep: Scotland was warmer then than it is today. The site was covered by wind-blown sand until the present century – a means of preservation it shares with the better-known Skara Brae on mainland Orkney.

In time, other wanderers blended into the racial mix. These early folk left traces of grave goods and different styles of burial, and the awesome monuments that provide clues to their spiritual life. These include powerful presences such as the Standing Stones of Callanish on the Island of Lewis – a site second in importance only to Stonehenge in England.

The first Celts

 Around 500 BC a new group of settlers or invaders arrived in Scotland – the earliest Celts. They arrived with new weapon technology and superior metal-working skills from north-west Europe. They seem to have overrun or subjugated the folk they found, even displacing their language by what is today described by linguists as P-Celtic because of the prevalence of consonants formed by the lips, such as 'p', 'b', 'v'. They called themselves Pretani, and this was later recorded by the Romans as 'Britons' when, about five centuries on, the legions came in strength to subdue the north.

The Romans in Scotland

The Romans found the area split into tribal sections. Experienced campaigners, they built forts, main and subsidiary, to control the conquered territories. By AD 80 Agricola, the Roman commander, had consolidated the gains by placing forts along the Forth–Clyde 'waist' of Scotland and by AD 82, after further reconnaissance, he had moved north up the east coast, where the terrain was easier. Supply ships went with him. Eventually, by AD 83, he had scouted through the central Highlands into the lower grounds of Moray, Nairn and the valley of the Spey, where the scant remains of marching camps survive to this day. His campaign was recorded by Tacitus, a Roman historian, who uses the term 'Caledonia' to describe the land north of the Forth and Clyde.

The first battle in Scotland

Then in the late summer of AD 83 Roman forces learned of a concentration of Caledonians under a leader named Calcagus, gathered on a hill called Mons Graupius. The Romans gave battle and their professional soldiers and superior cavalry defeated the native tribes. This is Scotland's first re-corded battle, yet one which has never been precisely located. Current thinking favours a site near Aberdeenshire's Bennachie, fitting in with Tacitus' description of a hill in the far north in sight of the sea. A Roman marching camp has been located nearby, but probably the exact site of this first battle will forever be a mystery.

Some 1,400 years later, Tacitus' biography of Agricola was printed and an early typesetter misread Graupius as Grampius. Hence the name Grampian – familiar to north-east Scots – should really be Graupian.

Beyond the northern wall

Rebellions in other parts of the empire ensured the Romans did not capitalise on their victory. Though they established a network of forts, especially in Tayside (where Inchtuthil was the main one), these were gradually abandoned for a line much further to the south between the Tyne and the Solway. Known as Hadrian's Wall, this frontier defence was a stone and turf wall with a fort every 1½ km (1 mile). They returned in AD 142–3 to build the Antonine Wall along the narrow Forth–Clyde line. This was a turf wall, underpinned by stone, with a fort every 3 km (2 miles).

Roman occupation ebbed and flowed, depending on military needs in other parts of their empire. They pulled back to Hadrian's Wall sometime around AD 160–70 but returned in punitive expeditions in AD 209. For many decades afterwards, the Caledonians (or Picti, as the Latin writers began to call them, meaning painted men, because they coloured their bodies) remained troublesome. In a sense, both the Antonine Wall and

Pages 10–11:
Suilven, from the Norse sul *and Gaelic* bheinn, *meaning pillar-mountain, is a great block of Torridonian sandstone lying on top of a glacier-scoured plinth of Lewissian gneiss. It looks spectacular from every angle.*

13

the more substantial Hadrian's Wall to the south were firebreaks, to prevent the linking up of rebellious tribes in the uplands all around. It was to be many centuries before a real frontier between the as yet unformed countries of Scotland and England was fixed.

The Scots arrive

Within 100 years of the Roman withdrawal, a new wave of settlers moved into the western seaboard of present-day Argyll or Strathclyde, whose presence took the formation of Scotland much nearer. They were the Scots. Their language, like the tribes there before them, was Celtic in origin; we call it Q-Celtic, because of the use of hard consonants like 'c', 'g' or 'kw' (hence Q). This became Gaelic. (P-Celtic became Welsh.) The Scots landed, settled, prospered and advanced, which brought them into conflict with Pictish tribes of central and northern Scotland. The first kingdom of the Scots was called Dalriada, a name transferred from their original home in Ireland (the term means king's court), and was founded in the south-west.

Christianity in Scotland

One other factor was at work in shaping the origins of the Scottish kingdom, and this was Christianity. The first Christians in Scotland were Romans; the first known native-born Christian was St Ninian, a Briton from the Solway area. Around AD 400 he founded a church, called in Latin Candida Casa (the white house) at the Christian community of Whithorn. (This may have been founded independently, or possibly was an offshoot of a Roman foundation elsewhere.) The full story is told in today's Whithorn Visitor Centre where a programme of excavation in the 1980s around the surviving twelfth-century priory confirmed the site as the real cradle of Christianity in Scotland.

Scottish Christianity is also associated with the tiny island of Iona, lying just west of the much larger island of Mull. It was to here that St Columba came. A high-born man of the Irish kingdom of Dalriada (that is, the original home of the Scots) he arrived in 'Scottish Dalriada' in 563 on a mission to convert the Picts – hitherto enemies of the Scots – to Christianity. The mission prospered, and a shared religion brought close links with the Picts in the north and the Britons to the south.

The Scots and the Picts

Thus by Columba's time there were three tribes of Celtic origin – Britons, Picts and Scots – living in what was to become Scotland. Around the same time, another wave of settlers arrived from what is today's Germany and the Low Countries. Now collectively known as Anglo-Saxons, they settled throughout England, eventually reaching its north-west coast so that the

Opposite: Perhaps one of the last symbol stones to be carved in the Grampian area, the Maiden Stone, near Bennachie, is an impressive ninth-century work. The tough granite has been worked simply and skilfully and shows typical Pictish symbols on both sides, including a Pictish beast and a double comb and mirror on the lower two panels of the side illustrated here.

15

original Britons in Strathclyde and Galloway were separated from their cousins in Wales. This situation remains to this day.

Eventually, in northern England, kingdoms and sub-kingdoms were set up from a Northumbrian power base with rule extending north of the River Tweed, into the Lothians around Edinburgh. Thus to the original three Scottish kingdoms of Pictland, Dalriada (the Scots) and the Strathclyde Britons, there was added a non-Celtic area.

Anglo-Saxon incursion was checked by the Picts at the mighty battle in 689 at Nechtansmere near Forfar in Angus. Little is known about it but it was certainly a Celt against non-Celt encounter, perhaps even – loosely speaking – the first Scots v. English match. But not only were these Pictish tribes assailed from the south and the west (as the Dalriadian kingdom applied pressure), they also faced the most terrifying enemy in northern Europe – the Vikings.

Some say the Norsemen came as settlers, others as destroyers and pillagers. More permanent occupiers followed in the wake of the warriors. They were impartial in their attacks. Not only the northern Picts suffered but also Scots and Britons on the western seaboard; the Christian settlement at Iona was also repeatedly attacked. In 839, after the Picts were badly mauled by these fierce seaborne folk, the Scots king, Kenneth Macalpine, saw his chance to extend north and eastwards into the territories of his weakened Celtic cousins. By 843 he was King of Scots *and* Picts. This new kingdom was known as Alba.

For the next 150 years Kenneth's descendants won or lost the crown of this northern kingdom by tactics in variety both fair and foul. Allegiances were made and abandoned in a sometimes bloody power struggle. Around 920, for example, King Constantine III made allies of the Northumbrians in order to check Norse incursions, only to change sides in order to try to eject English settlement in the Lothians. In 1016 King Malcolm II decisively defeated the Northumbrians at the Battle of Carham near Coldstream and Scotland's barrier was fixed along the River Tweed where it remains today.

Norman influence in Scotland

Somewhere in all this, in the year 1040, a certain King Duncan was murdered by his own general, Macbeth, who took the throne and thereby provided the plot, about five and a half centuries later, for one of the greatest of William Shakespeare's tragedies. Macbeth in turn was deposed by King Malcolm III, often known as Canmore, meaning great chief (literally, in Gaelic, big head). As was to happen many times, the futures of Scotland and England became intertwined after the marriage of the same Malcolm to Margaret, granddaughter of England's Edward the Confessor. She had become a refugee following the Norman Conquest of England in 1066.

Margaret's legacy in Scotland was far-reaching. Her piety led later to her canonisation, but her influence on her Celtic warrior husband was very strong. Even the location of his court was changed, from Dunfermline to Edinburgh, in the more 'anglicised' Lothians. Margaret's own chapel survives today by the battlements of Edinburgh Castle as the oldest building to be seen in Scotland's capital. Her name is also recalled in North and South Queensferry, a ferry service she created specifically for pilgrims north-bound for St Andrews.

From Margaret's time onwards, contact with England meant dealing with the Norman methods of government and social order now in place there. Before long, Scotland was introduced to the feudal system, the granting of land by the king in exchange for military service. Though there was resistance to this process, by the time of King David I (1124–53) there was a measure of peace and stability in the young nation. David, one of Malcolm's sons, had been educated in the Norman manner and proceeded to model state and government on Norman methods, welcoming and settling in Scotland Norman families with names such as Comyn and Graham and, significantly, de-Brus or Bruce. He also introduced a proper system of coinage and minting. (To this day, Scottish banknotes differ from those of England. The Royal Bank of Scotland is the only bank now producing £1 notes in the UK. The Bank of England's £1 coin is unpopular in Scotland – sometimes referred to dismissively as a foreign coin, with many Scots shoppers positively asking for the note instead of the coin in change. However, English money of any denomination is accepted at face value in Scotland.)

Early skirmishing leads to uneasy peace

Through marriage with the daughter of an English earl, King David had gained lands in Huntingdon in England. As he thereby became the Earl of Huntingdon, he had, in the Norman manner, ceremonially to bow his knee to the King of England and hence acknowledge him as overlord. Earlier kings had done the same, reinforcing the English belief – the Scots would say misapprehension – that the Scots were thereby vassals of the supreme English king. However, in David's time, Scotland was left in peace as a now united kingdom already forging links with Europe in trade and diplomacy.

Unfortunately, this happy position did not remain for long. David's grandson, King William 'The Lion', joined English barons in a revolt against King Henry II of England. (William had hoped to gain Northumbria as reward for his support, demonstrating it was not just the kings of England who had expansionist plans.) His venture went hopelessly wrong in a series of battles near the border. In 1174 he was captured and the English king compelled him to swear allegiance. This he did at

Falaise in Normandy, and the Treaty of Falaise reinforced ever after the English Crown's belief in its feudal superiority. Later, Richard I ('the Lionheart') of England revoked the treaty for cash – in effect selling back Scotland's independence – because he needed money for a crusade.

Scotland's 'Golden Age'

If Scotland had any kind of 'Golden Age' then it could be said to have been in the time of King Alexander III. He married a daughter of King Henry III of England, and while the thorny question of overlordship remained an issue, Alexander's skilful political management gave Scotland a long era of relative peace and prosperity.

In later decades of his long reign, Alexander even managed to settle the Norwegian question. The Norse still occupied the Western Isles as a possible launching platform for mainland expansion. Alexander instigated needling attacks by his northern lords, rousing the warlike King Haakon to retaliate. The result was the prolonged skirmish of the Battle of Largs on the Clyde coast in 1263. The Norse retired to their homeland and in 1266 the Western Isles finally became, through treaty, part of Scotland. Scotland's relationship with Norway improved thereafter and the cordial atmosphere was further strengthened by the marriage of Alexander's daughter Margaret into the Norwegian royal family. Even relations with England improved – after all, Alexander was the son-in-law of the English king.

But times moved on. King Edward I of England came to the throne, keen to expand his kingdom. Both the sons of Alexander died and his married daughter Margaret also, leaving Alexander's infant granddaughter in Norway as the heir to the throne. With the future of Scotland insecure, Alexander remarried, this time to the high-born Frenchwoman Yolande de Dreux, in 1285.

A fall in darkness

Opposite: Often called the cradle of Scottish Christianity, the religious settlement on the island of Iona was founded by St Columba, an Irish monk, with 12 followers in AD 563. Often the target of Norse raids, the Abbey and its associated buildings later fell into decay. Restoration work started early in the twentieth century. Iona was the burial place of the early kings of Scotland.

There are times in Scotland's story when some random chance of good or ill causes a major turning point in the nation's fate. Such a time was a bleak March afternoon in 1286. On the completion of a council in Edinburgh, Alexander decided, against all advice, to ride back to his new wife at Kinghorn, on the other side of the Forth. He rode to South Queensferry and persuaded the ferryman to take him across in the teeth of a gale. He safely reached the northern shore in darkness and with local guides and retainers set off eastwards. Somewhere near Kinghorn, where green cliffs run down to the sea, his horse stumbled. Alexander died from the fall.

Alexander was perhaps the best king ever to reign in Scotland and his death changed Scotland's course forever. However, he left a nation-state which was stable and strong and which acted responsibly faced with the problems of succession brought about by his unexpected death. Six guardians were put in charge until such time as Alexander's grand-daughter, Margaret of Norway, was old enough to be crowned.

The Hammer of the Scots

King Edward I of England, as Margaret's great-uncle, was asked for advice and he suggested marrying his son to Margaret as soon as both were old enough, thereby guaranteeing harmony between the two kingdoms. A treaty was signed accordingly but three months later the child Margaret died on her way to Scotland.

There were now many claimants to the throne. In good faith, the Guardians of Scotland once more turned to Edward as arbiter. He declared that before he chose he would require acknowledgement of his own claim to be the overlord of Scotland. All 13 claimants all too readily agreed to Edward's request. Balancing various claims of nearness through blood links and seniority, Edward chose John Balliol. Edward required various acts of obedience from the new king, derisively called Toom Tabard (empty coat) by his subjects at home. In 1295 Edward pushed Balliol too far, ordering him to join him in a French war. Instead, Balliol renounced his allegiance and sided with France, thereby creating the first of the Franco-Scottish strategic and military links which eventually came to be called the Auld Alliance. This led Scotland continually to side with France against the common enemy of England, a disastrous foreign policy which was to bedevil Scotland for the next three centuries.

Edward promptly invaded Scotland and destroyed Balliol's army at Dunbar in 1296. The Earl of Surrey was placed in charge of the occupying forces, while the once-powerful families of Scotland, with their substantial land holdings, hurried to secure their goods and gear by signing a document swearing allegiance to Edward. It was later to be dismissively called the Ragman's Roll from its tattered appearance, festooned with the seals of Scottish nobility. Amongst the booty which Edward took homewards was the Cross of St Margaret (with its fragment of the true cross), much of the nation's records and archives and also the Stone of Destiny on which generations of Scottish kings had been crowned.

The Stone of Destiny

The loss of this part of the nation's fabric is keenly felt by some nationalists to this day. It is still kept in Westminster Abbey, though some argue that the Westminster Stone is not the original. It was even snatched and taken temporarily back to Scotland by young patriots as recently as 1950. Or was it? This ordinary-looking piece of sandstone has given rise to a most romantic, yet beguilingly plausible tale. On hearing the approach of Edward, it is suggested, the monks of the Abbey of Scone had time to hide the real stone and substitute a flawed block cast aside in a nearby quarry. Few knew what the real stone looked like. Moreover the Stone is a completely different shape from that shown on contemporary seals.

This most powerful symbol of Scotland was hidden away by the monks in a chamber in Dunsinane Hill, three miles from Scone. There it was discovered by two young farmhands in 1800. In 1818 excavators found a very large stone of meteoric origin along with two engraved tablets. At that time interest in Scottish heritage was at a low ebb and the stone was shipped to London for examination. After that it disappeared. Perhaps at a time of political unease, the authorities found it 'hot' property and liable to awaken old hopes. Could this stone, imbued with the power to protect the kingdom, still lie forgotten and unrecognised in a garden or graveyard in the bustling English capital?

 TWO

INDEPENDENT
SCOTLAND

After 1296, King Edward of England's policy seemed to be the dismantling of the nation of Scotland and to this end English officials were placed in charge of his new territory. Yet resistance was not wholly crushed. The earliest of Scotland's freedom fighters against the forces of occupation was William Wallace. By 1297 Wallace is known to have been skirmishing with a small band and he had already been declared an outlaw by the English king. His most famous victory was on Stirling Bridge, in that same year, when an extraordinary tactical error by the English forces holding Stirling Castle allowed Wallace and his army to destroy them as they crossed the narrow bridge over the Forth in order to give battle. Wallace became Guardian of Scotland and made diplomatic contact with European powers in an attempt to restore Scotland's role as a free-trading nation. Edward, now more determined than ever to annihilate what he perceived as a terrorist threat, took a huge army north. He cornered Wallace's forces at Falkirk and defeated them, first using archers at long range to thin out the Scottish spearmen. Lacking the heavy cavalry needed against the bowmen, Wallace could do little.

As an ordinary Scot, Wallace did not command the resources to secure the aristocratic grand knights and their heavy horses and weaponry: in simple terms he could not buy the hardware to win back the kingdom. Though he escaped from Falkirk to continue diplomatic efforts in Europe and guerrilla warfare in Scotland, he was eventually betrayed in 1305. He died defiant, spurning all offers of reconciliation in his efforts to secure Scotland's unconditional independence. He was in consequence tortured and dismembered, to a recipe personally thought up by Edward.

Robert the Bruce

Though Wallace had been popular with everyday folk, several of Scotland's aristocratic families had stood back and watched, perhaps waiting for their own opportunity. Among the watchers was Robert the Bruce. Bruce had had close contact with the English throne throughout this time,

Strategic fortress and royal court of the Stewart monarchs, Stirling Castle was the final prize in the Scots Wars of Independence. Because of its position as the lowest bridging point on the River Forth, with marshes to the west and high ground above and below, Stirling Castle controlled all routes across the narrow 'waist' of Scotland between the Highlands and Lowlands.

as his father had been one of the original 13 claimants of the Scottish crown. He certainly represented one political faction in Scotland, while John Comyn (nephew of 'Toom Tabard' Balliol) was his most powerful rival. Comyn and Bruce were for a time seen as joint Guardians of Scotland, and their families formed an uneasy band of possible conspirators in the murky context of English court politics. Bruce's hand was forced in 1306, perhaps because John Comyn leaked news of rebellion plans. Comyn and Bruce met in the Greyfriars Church in Dumfries, where they quarrelled, Comyn receiving a fatal stab wound. This event precipitated Bruce's own ambitions and he was crowned king at Scone in 1307. The seven-year road which led to the decisive Battle of Bannockburn involved much bloodshed and setbacks, but Bruce was of royal blood and could call on resources never available to the 'folk hero' Wallace.

The Battle of Bannockburn

The most important date in Scotland's history is the easy-to-remember 1314, the date of the Battle of Bannockburn, when that rarest of affairs in Scottish history occurred – a victory against England. Many Scots today are hard pressed to recall the dates of the many defeats that followed:

Halidon Hill, Flodden (most terrible of all), Solway Moss or Pinkie, amongst others, but Bannockburn is always remembered. Even today, nationalists rally there on the anniversary of the battle, a midsummer day in June. Thus its emotional force is still strong, its significance translated into a modern visitor attraction in the care of the National Trust for Scotland.

Incongruously, this is no Culloden on a dark and moody moor or Killiecrankie amidst the drama of a wooded highland pass – just two other places where dramatic battles took place. Bannockburn today is a thoroughly ordinary suburb of Stirling. Everyday housing, schools and commercial buildings cover the area. However, when Scotland's King Robert I, most familiarly called Robert the Bruce, surveyed the ground, he found it marshy and low lying, running gently towards the widening River Forth. With its pools and soft places it was difficult ground on which King Edward of England would be hard pressed to deploy effectively the iron fist of his forces, the heavy-armoured knights. Having learned the lesson of Falkirk, Bruce's light cavalry was able to prevent effective use of English archery; then his blocks of spearmen were able to push and hold the heavy cavalry, impaling them in a boggy area, too small for the armoured knights to manoeuvre, between the winding River Forth and the cleft of the Bannock Burn. This was to be a key to the smaller Scots army's success. The story is told in the NTS visitor centre by means of an audio-visual programme and a fascinatingly detailed wall panorama. Thus, out of the muddy gore of Bannockburn where the flower of English chivalry died in the marshy pools, Scotland once again was made free of domination.

Bruce won his kingdom back by force of arms, and blood was spilled repeatedly along the Scottish borders in the years that followed. King Robert even appealed to the Pope (hitherto a firm believer in England's divine right to rule Scotland). Scottish churchmen, towards the close of the thirteenth century, had been firmly nationalist, presenting the intellectual argument for Scotland's separateness. They had supported Bruce throughout his campaign. Now they came together in Arbroath Abbey in 1320 and produced perhaps the best-known document in Scotland's history: the Declaration of Arbroath. It contains the famous lines

For so long as a hundred of us shall remain alive we shall never accept subjection to the domination of the English. For we fight not for glory, or riches or honour, but for freedom alone which no good man will consent to lose but with his life.

Interestingly, the declaration also makes reference to the acknowledgement of a king as a symbolic leader only as long as he stands for the best interests of the nation. The Scots of the fourteenth century were already, it seems, wary of the notion that rights to rule were granted only through divine powers to the exclusion of the wishes of the people. Finally, in 1328, England wearied of the border squabbles and temporarily abandoned all claims to overlordship.

A perilous freedom

Yet Scotland did not advance to harmonious prosperity. King Robert's death in 1329 saw an all-too-frequently repeated situation: a child crowned and a regent in charge. The expansionist hopes of the English court were once again kindled. In 1332, Edward III sent an army north which included disinherited or otherwise displeased Scots, and defeated the Scots at Dupplin Moor and at Halidon Hill near Berwick-upon-Tweed in 1333.

Scotland returned to conflict in 1346, invading England in support of the French. Inevitably the Scots were defeated at Neville's Cross near Durham, where King David II was captured. He was a prisoner of the English for 13 years, at the end of which a huge ransom was paid. On his death in 1371, the succession moved sideways to a nephew, Robert Stewart – the son of Marjorie, daughter of Robert the Bruce.

From Robert II descended the Stewart (or French-style Stuart) monarchs of Scotland. Often endowed with charismatic personalities, the Stewart kings were largely not blessed with political acumen, and Scotland often paid a heavy price for their lack of judgement.

Robert's son King James I (of Scotland) was captured as a boy on his way to France for safekeeping in 1406 and was in English hands until 1424, though after his release he ruled Scotland well until he was conspiratorially murdered in 1437. James II also met a violent end; he was killed by a bursting cannon while besieging Roxburgh Castle.

The Lords of the Isles

James III, his successor in 1460, hit upon the policy of diverting some of the court schemers in a strategy to subdue the Western Isles – for while Scotland's story was played out in a Lowland court, the Highland clans had themselves been busy. Until very recently, the Highlands were an unknown territory to most Lowland folk. Language and geography combined to form a substantial barrier. It was not surprising, therefore, that the Gaels had gradually developed a semi-autonomous kingdom of their own, supporting the Scottish monarchy only when it suited them.

The most powerful Gaelic leaders were the Lords of the Isles, the mighty Clan Donald. In 1461 the Lord of the Isles even made an independent treaty with the English King Edward IV.

In James III's time, therefore, a powerful Gaelic political and cultural identity had developed. This continued to influence the political strategy of Clan Donald two centuries later. But by 1476 the Scots Crown had contained the threat for the time being, though rebellions from various factions within the clan continued for almost another century. Yet, for all James III's efforts to consolidate authority, he lost his life attempting to quell rebellion from his own nobles. After the Battle of Sauchieburn, near Falkirk, in 1488, he fell from his horse. The priest who was called to the scene drew a knife and murdered him.

Flodden and Solway Moss

King James IV brought stability to his country but revived the French alliance. While the English King Henry VIII was campaigning against the French, James was able to rally all of the Scottish nobility. The result was that in 1513 an army – some say 20,000 strong – crossed the border, only to be destroyed by a force under the Earl of Surrey at Flodden Field. On the day of the battle James threw away the tactical advantage of high ground while the English employed artillery with deadly effect. James was cut down like a common soldier and his body was carried off in triumph to England.

The next king, James V, was, like so many Stewarts before and after him, only an infant (18 months old) when he succeeded to the throne. He grew up eventually to rule and made two French marriages, stubbornly supporting the French cause against the English and hence causing a split amongst the Scottish nobility. Finally, in 1542, and in a repetition of events earlier in the century, he took an army south, only to be defeated at Solway Moss. Devastated, James returned home, eventually arriving at his favourite hunting lodge, Falkland Palace. There news was brought of the birth of a daughter. As a final comment on the Stewart dynasty, James is reported to have said that it came with a lass (through Marjorie, Robert the Bruce's daughter) and would go with a lass. A week later he died. The now fatherless child was Mary, Queen of Scots.

The story of Mary, Queen of Scots

The story of Mary, Queen of Scots is part of a larger drama of political and religious strife, acted out in the royal houses of Scotland, France and England. In her seven-year reign she became perhaps the most fascinating and enigmatic of all the characters in Scotland's story.

Political and religious division

Mary's birth coincided with a period of great political and religious uncertainty in Europe. The Reformation movement in the sixteenth century had

25

Previous page: *This once magnificent palace lies ruined on a site overlooking Linlithgow Loch. Though a fortified site since early times, nothing visible today predates a fire of 1424 – and the palace met its end in another fire in 1746 when it was burned, probably by accident, when occupied by government troops under General Hawley. Linlithgow Palace's most famous occupant was Mary, Queen of Scots. She was born here in 1542.*

convulsed many nations by its stance against the political power of the Catholic Church. In Scotland, already experiencing the first shock-waves of the Reformation, two parties struggled for power. The Protestant Reformers favoured an alliance with Henry VIII of England, a vigorous opponent of Catholicism who had cast aside papal authority and dissolved the monasteries in 1534. The other party, the supporters of the Roman Catholic Church, looked towards France where Catholicism was still strong. Mary's mother, Mary of Guise, was of the French royal house. With a Catholic Scots monarch of French descent, France and its church expected Scotland to side with them against Henry VIII – the Auld Alliance activated once more.

Disquieted by the prospect of this, King Henry demanded that Mary be brought to England. He wanted to marry off his own son Edward (the future King Edward VI of England) to the infant Mary as soon as possible to remove the threat she would otherwise pose – and, before Mary was three years old, he had sent an army to back his claim, in an episode known as the 'Rough Wooing'.

In such a confused political situation, plots and counter-plots were rife. One resulted in the murder of the pro-French Cardinal Beaton who, along with James Hamilton, Earl of Arran, and Mary of Guise, ruled Scotland for the infant queen. St Andrews Castle, his headquarters, was captured by a pro-Reformation faction, including John Knox, the fiery leader of the Reformation movement. In 1547 the castle fell again, this time to a French force, and Knox himself was taken and made a galley-slave. Though Henry VIII had meanwhile died, English forces again crossed the border, and defeated the Scots at Pinkie near Musselburgh.

The English invaders followed a policy of maximum destruction as an army of occupation. Many Scots did not know which way to turn. Though they did not like Catholicism, they liked the English forces who represented the Protestant cause even less! Nationalist feeling ran high and the Scots appealed to the French for help in ridding their country of the English armies. The French in turn put pressure on English forces in France and the result was an English withdrawal from Scotland. The price was the removal of Mary from Scotland to France. She sailed from Dumbarton for France in 1548 – a six-year-old over whom there had already been much bloodshed.

Over the next 10 years, Scotland moved more towards support of France's foreign policy. There were Frenchmen in high office within Scotland and even the former Governor, Arran, had been awarded the French Duchy of Chatelherault for his part in the removal of Mary to France. With France now at war with England, highly trained French troops garrisoned Scottish fortresses.

Queen of France

Scotland and France seemed to cement their relationship with the marriage of Mary to the Dauphin (Crown Prince) Francis in 1558. The following year she became Queen of France when her husband became King Francis II. However, at the end of 1560, he died, leaving Mary a childless widow at the age of 17. Had they produced children, these descendants would have ruled France and Scotland jointly, giving even more substance to the Auld Alliance.

Mary became isolated in France. In the same sad year of 1560 in which she had lost her husband, her mother, Mary of Guise, also died. The Guise family's influence weakened in the French court which was now dominated by Catharine de' Medici, the Queen Mother. Clearly, there was no role for Mary, except that of a teenage dowager, so she returned to Scotland in 1561.

Mary in Scotland

The religious divide in Scotland had been growing ever wider. Though John Knox, architect of the Reformation, preached sermons against her from Edinburgh's St Giles Kirk, Mary cleverly showed religious tolerance. She hoped to make peace with the Scottish Protestants while keeping links with the Catholic powers in Europe. Her personal attributes of beauty, great presence and liking for open-air pursuits helped her in this delicate balancing act. She won popularity with the ordinary folk who saw her as she travelled through her kingdom: Fife in the spring each year 1562–6; summer visits to Inverness and Aberdeen in 1562–4; Argyll and Ayrshire during the summer of 1563; autumn excursions through the south-west in 1565–6. Though the Palace of Holyroodhouse was her headquarters, she often visited Stirling Castle.

Mary cannot be placed just in a Scottish setting. She was next in line to succeed Elizabeth of England if the latter died childless. Elizabeth, however, neither recognised Mary as her successor nor seemed to have any intentions of marrying and producing an heir. Catholic politicians cast around Europe, trying to find Mary a Catholic husband; yet, at the same time, politicians on both sides of the border tried to find Mary a Protestant husband, as this would strengthen the Anglo-Scottish relationship. Elizabeth even proposed the Earl of Leicester, though rumours were rife that she herself was having a scandalous affair with him! Once again, Mary's marriage prospects were the subject of powerful political manipulation.

Mary and Lord Darnley

However, Mary took matters into her own hands when she met Lord Darnley. A member of the Lennox family, he was closely related to both the English and Scottish royal houses – in any case, Mary had totally fallen for the dubious charms of this languid young man, four years her junior. She described him as 'the lustiest and best proportioned lang man' that she had ever met. Their marriage in 1564 in the Chapel Royal of Holyrood was followed by 'balling, and dancing, and banqueting' for the next three days, as a disapproving John Knox wrote at the time.

A more important result was the split of Scotland's most powerful families into separate factions. The House of Hamilton, that is, the Earl of Arran (Chatelherault), raised a rebellion, along with the Earl of Moray, another figure hitherto enjoying influence at Mary's court. However, their activities were easily suppressed by Mary and her supporters, with the young queen, glowing and triumphant, riding at the head of her troops.

Historians have described Darnley in a range of terms from dull to morally worthless. He was also arrogant, impetuous and very fond of slipping out of the Palace of Holyroodhouse for an evening's carousing in the taverns of the Royal Mile! Though she showered him with titles and trinkets, Mary soon had little in common with her husband. She excluded him from any real power and regal authority at her court in Holyroodhouse. Mary tended to favour those towards whom she felt personal warmth, rather than political allegiance. Soon, other lords in high office also began to feel disenchanted. Their resentment focused on David Riccio, musician and Secretary to the Queen, whom they felt exercised too much political influence on her. The mean-natured and ever-jealous Darnley suspected worse and together the lords plotted to murder this Italian usurper of the Queen's attention. According to contemporary accounts, Riccio was ugly, small and hunched, even if he could sing well and play the lute, and it is unlikely there was a shred of truth in any insinuation of an affair.

Riccio was murdered by Darnley and the conspirators before the queen's horrified eyes. Mary herself believed that this violent incident betrayed intentions to threaten her own life. She immediately set to work repairing her relationship with Darnley, thus detaching him from the conspirators. Her son James was born in 1566 and baptised in the Catholic faith, which the Scottish Protestants viewed with alarm. The reconciliation failed, however, and she found herself attracted to James Hepburn, Earl of Bothwell. The year 1567 was one of the most critical in Scottish history. Mary had already pardoned the murderers of Riccio, in the hope that they might assist in the removal of Darnley. She rewarded various Protestant ministers, as if looking for support in an impending crisis. She probably knew of plots to 'eliminate' her estranged husband.

Bothwell and defeat

The events of early 1567 are still a matter of dispute. At some point, Mary became pregnant again, probably by Bothwell. Whatever the truth, she attempted to improve matters between herself and Darnley. Yet Darnley met an obscure end in the garden of the Kirk o' Field, close by Holyrood, where he was recovering from illness. The house in which he was convalescing blew up in a huge explosion and Darnley's body was found, unmarked by the blast, in the garden some distance away. He had been strangled.

Though many parties – Mary, the Riccio conspirators and many Scottish politicians – wanted the unpopular Darnley out of the way, his murder remains the most enduring mystery in Scottish history. It made possible the queen's marriage to Bothwell, who was acquitted of Darnley's murder

Opposite, far right: Many portraits of Mary exist though several date from the seventeenth and eighteenth centuries and so are not authentic. This portrait was painted in 1578, during her period in captivity, by Peter Oudrey, an otherwise unrecorded artist.

Opposite, top left: Mary married the Dauphin François in 1558 when he was 14 and she only 15. The following year he became King of France, but died before reaching 17. This portrait is attributed to Leonard Limosin I.

Opposite, middle left: Henry Stewart, Lord Darnley was Mary's second husband. He was a member of the powerful Catholic family, the Stewarts of Lennox. This portrait by Hans Eworth was painted in 1555 and shows Darnley when about 9 years old.

Opposite, bottom left: A miniature believed to be of Mary's third husband, James Hepburn, the Fourth Earl of Bothwell. After the mysterious death of her second husband, she married Bothwell in 1567, though their union lasted only a month.

MARIA
D   G
SCOTIA
PIISSIMA REGINA
FRANCIA DOTARIA
ANNO
ÆTATIS REGNIQ
36
ANGLICA CAPTIVIT
10
S   H
1578

and promptly divorced his own wife. For Mary to agree to so swift a marriage would have been unseemly, so she made weak protestations as Bothwell carried her by force to Dunbar Castle. Some historians believe that her pregnancy dated only from this episode, and explains her hasty third marriage rather than her attempted reconciliation with Darnley.

By marrying Bothwell (according to Protestant rites, this time), Mary did little for her own reputation. She had abandoned the Catholic Church, thus enabling the new church to gain in power and status. Yet again, Scotland's powerful families were split into opposing factions. A confederacy of senior men rose against Mary's latest liaison. The rebellion grew and its forces attacked Borthwick Castle, where Bothwell had taken his bride. They, in turn, escaped, raised what support they could and met the rebellious lords at Carberry, near Edinburgh. Surprisingly, no blood was spilt and, after a day of wrangling, Mary surrendered. Her impetuous relationship with Bothwell was over. Their marriage had lasted only a month and he ultimately died, insane, in a Danish prison.

Imprisonment, escape and imprisonment again

Mary was taken first to Edinburgh where crowds gathered to shout insults at her. Within two days she was imprisoned in Loch Leven Castle and there she later miscarried of twins. Yet even in her darkest hours in prison, she was not without support. Many in Scotland felt a deep-rooted reluctance to take the final step and strip a monarch of all power and authority.

Only a few months later, in May 1568, her supporters arranged her escape. All the ingredients of a melodrama were there: a brave young boy beguiled by the queen's charms, a stolen key and a romantic flight across the loch, while in disguise. The young lad was Willy Douglas, an orphaned cousin of the house of Douglas, in whose castle Mary was imprisoned. By sleight of hand he removed the key from his master the laird's pocket. The queen, disguised as a countrywoman, openly walked across the courtyard. Willy let her out, relocked the main gate and hid the keys in a nearby cannon. Minutes later, she was lying, out of sight, below the gunwales of a rowing boat, as her faithful supporters made for the shore.

Bishops, earls and lords gathered round her – a force of 5,000–6,000 men – and prepared for battle at Langside, near Glasgow. Facing them was the anti-Catholic faction, the Lords of the Congregation, who favoured her young son, the future King James VI. Though outnumbered on the battlefield at Langside, they showed the better military tactics and Mary's forces were defeated. Only 11 days after her escape from Loch Leven, Mary fled southwards, towards the Solway. She crossed into England, hoping for an audience with Queen Elizabeth which was never to take place. Without ever seeing Scotland again, Mary remained in captivity for nearly 20 years, a pawn in the political game played around her. With England still resisting Catholic attempts to regain power, Mary, as a focus for a possible French invasion, was finally implicated in a plot to place her on the English throne. Elizabeth signed her death warrant in 1587.

King James VI of Scotland

Mary, Queen of Scots, never saw her son after he was 10 months old. He became King of Scotland when he was 14 years old in 1581. He was to rule with cunning and political skill, choosing advisers of ability rather than nobility. Because of the changes brought about by the Reformation, he was also able to control the power of the church and its lands.

King James VI eventually succeeded to the English throne, becoming King James I of England, after Queen Elizabeth of England died childless. This was the so-called Union of the Crowns, in some ways a curious arrangement. James packed and headed for the bright lights of London, leaving the government of Scotland to its Privy Council. He returned only once, in 1617.

Religious wars

As the seventeenth century rolled on, religious controversy began to centre on the structure and powers of the reformed church in Scotland. James believed in a uniform Episcopacy – that is, a church controlled by bishops appointed by the king – whereas more radical Protestants favoured a Presbyterian system in which authority resided with elders of the church chosen by the congregation. This was the crucial issue of the religious wars that bedevilled Scotland and England in this century, and both sides adhered most fervently to their principles in a way that is hard for us to understand.

James' son Charles I took the throne on his father's death and inherited his belief in Episcopacy. He continued his father's attempts to assert this uniformity over the Presbyterian element in Scotland. The Scots reacted to his standardisation plans – involving, for example, a new prayer book – by rioting in 1637 and by creating a National Covenant. This was a document asserting that the right of appointment of churchmen was by the people – that is, God's will – as opposed to the king acting through his bishops, as in Episcopacy. By challenging the rights of the king to make law, the document implied that this was the prerogative of parliament.

The rise of the Covenanters

There was a great gathering in the Greyfriars Kirk and kirkyard in Edinburgh in February 1638 as earls and ordinary folk, ministers and military men queued to sign the National Covenant. Copies were sent out throughout Scotland. The result was a counter-proclamation by the king, though there were few means of enforcing it. By November a general

Son of Mary, Queen of Scots and Lord Darnley, James became King James VI of Scotland in 1581 following his mother's abdication. During his minority he was a pawn in the power struggle between various factions. Later he became embroiled in a long conflict with the Presbyterian Church – a struggle between Crown and Church which was to eventually lead to the downfall of the Stewarts. James succeeded to the throne of England in 1603 to become King James I as a descendant of King James IV and the English Margaret Tudor. This miniature of him was painted by Isaac Oliver.

assembly had revoked laws connected with Episcopacy and even condemned the bishops in their absence. These bold steps made civil war inevitable.

The Covenanting army soon controlled all of Scotland and there was a confrontation along the border with the army of King Charles. Though peace was finally agreed in June of 1639, mutual confidence was forever broken between the king and Scotland and in 1642, when the king and his English subjects seemed irreconcilable, the Covenanters aligned themselves with the English Parliamentary Party. The matter was settled by the execution of Charles I by the English Parliamentarians in 1649.

After the Restoration of King Charles II, son of the executed Charles I, in 1660, many of the Scottish aristocrats flocked to London to secure influential positions in government. Presbyterian ministers were turned out of the churches to make way for bishops and their curates. Armed confrontation was inevitable and thus came about the Covenanter Wars of 1666–90. The reign of Charles II ended with an uncontrolled army pillaging and imprisoning without quarter in one of Scotland's darkest hours. The accession of the Catholic King James VII (II of England) offered no improvement but the 'Glorious Revolution' was finally to overthrow James in 1688, after his second wife had produced a son, to continue the Catholic dynasty. Holland's ruler, William of Orange, who had married James VII's daughter Mary, accepted the invitation of English politicians to accede jointly with his wife to the throne. This precipitated two events in Scotland which are widely recalled today – the Battle of Killiecrankie and the Massacre of Glencoe.

'Whaur hae ye been sae braw, lad – Come ye by Killiecrankie O?'

Scotland had divided into two camps: those who supported the new order under William and Mary; and those who supported the exiled King James VII. The latter were henceforth known as Jacobites (from the Latin 'Jacobus' – James), a name which was to recur in Scotland's story for almost the next century. Battle between the two sides was inevitable and the opposing forces met at the dramatic Pass of Killiecrankie, a little way north of Pitlochry. Under the command of Viscount Dundee, the Jacobites allowed the royal army through the pass and then, late in the day, unleashed a Highland charge which proved irresistible, breaking the royalist ranks. However, in the very moment of triumph, a stray musket shot hit Dundee, who fell mortally wounded. Without his leadership, the campaign petered out.

The Massacre of Glencoe

If Killiecrankie has at least the romance of a leader slain in his moment of victory, it is difficult to portray the Massacre of Glencoe in any kind of romantic light. In 1691, the government proclaimed that all clan chiefs should take an oath of allegiance by the end of the year, or face trial for treason. They hoped to provoke resistance, providing an excuse to root out Jacobite clan chiefs once and for all. The Secretary of State for Scotland, Sir John Dalrymple of Stair, wrote to the commander of the local forces of government, Captain Robert Campbell of Glenlyon: 'I assure you your power shall be full enough, and I hope the soldiers will not trouble the government with prisoners.'

Most clan chiefs fell into line, but the chief of one minor sept of the MacDonalds of Glencoe, Alisdair MacDonald, called MacIain, was late journeying from his homeland in Glencoe to the magistrate to take the oath. Fierce blizzards delayed him and the sheriff-deputy was absent from the town of Inveraray when the chief arrived. This was enough. The Campbell militia entered the glen early in February and asked for quarters from the clan, which were freely given. On the thirteenth day of the month they then turned on their hosts, although they bungled the attempt at complete destruction. MacIain was murdered in his own bed-chamber and with him 36 of his men and a few women and children. The rest escaped into the snowy hills.

The same clan had previously looted Glenlyon (home of the troops' leader) giving the Clan Campbell, serving the government, little enough reason to feel sympathy for the MacDonalds. Nevertheless, the crux of the episode lies in the betrayal of trust. In the Highlands, food and shelter would always be given even to bitter enemies should these be requested and this code of honour between guest and host had been violated. The matter was made worse not only through the duplicity of Dalrymple of Stair, but by the fact that the king had authorised the betrayal, thereby tainting his own hands. The later parliamentary enquiry forced Stair to resign, but conveniently left out the king in its condemnation. Campbell and MacDonald were made enemies while the Jacobites were presented with useful propaganda.

Scotland and the age of commerce

Even before the end of the seventeenth century there were the first signs of an increasingly mercantile age which would soon dawn. Scotland was a poor country and wished to emulate the already apparent success of England in trading with the New World. Carried on a wave of nationalist sentiment, individual merchants, burghs and trade associations, as well as the nation's aristocracy, subscribed to a parliamentary proposal to found a Scottish colony overseas.

The venture was at first also open to merchants in England and Holland who were not a part of England's powerful and profitable East India Company. However, shareholders of the East India Company petitioned the king to forbid any English (or Dutch) merchant from participating in Scotland's venture. Thus England's influence ensured that Scotland found no other trading partners.

A colony was proposed on the Gulf of Darien on the Isthmus of Panama. In the euphoria surrounding the venture, no one considered that the area was torrid, wet and fever-ridden. It had been chosen as a key point in the Americas and *en route* to the Orient. Funds from home, from small merchants and powerful landowners alike, were soon forthcoming.

In 1698 the first of the Scottish ships reached their destination but the colony was doomed to disaster. Many of the colonists had died on the voyage, while even the natural harbour the colony had chosen to settle by proved difficult and dangerous to enter. The Scots leaders quarrelled amongst themselves and, more importantly, the land was claimed by Spain, which had colonies nearby. After Spanish attacks, during which England forbade her American colonies to aid the Scots, the colonists were forced to surrender. In 1700 the colony was abandoned.

Some say this was the worst ever disaster for Scotland, more significant than any battlefield defeat. Two thousand died in the attempt to emulate England's mercantile success; equally seriously, it left Scotland impoverished and vulnerable. The nation, encouraged by the Jacobites, rose in anger, petitioning the Scottish Parliament which moved resolutions blaming England for its role in the affair.

The loss of independence

In 1702 King William died, whereupon the crown of both nations passed to Anne (Mary's sister). None of Anne's children survived her, and on her death the English Parliament chose the Electress Sophia of Hanover – a granddaughter of King James VI – without consulting the Scots Parliament. The Scots Parliament, smarting from what they saw as high-handed dealings from the English Parliament and also still bitter about the Darien episode, demanded equal trading privileges if they also were to accept her – English power having created an overseas trading monopoly which the Scots had so far failed to breach. The implication was that the Scots could always declare as successor the 'Old Pretender' (James, son of James VII) who was waiting in Europe.

To this provocative political move England retaliated with economic sanctions, proclaiming that unless Scotland was prepared to accept the English Parliament's views on the accession, no Scot could inherit property in England (which alarmed the Scots aristocracy) and that there would be a total trade embargo on all Scottish goods. As impoverished Scotland had become dangerously dependent on England for trade, this was a threat which would have ruined Scotland utterly.

The situation of two Parliaments and one crown had become inherently unstable, and when England again became embroiled in a war with France, the risk of the pro-French Jacobites achieving power in Scotland was unacceptable. Using the incentive of free trade – on which the prosperity of many ordinary Scots depended – together with a series of personal rewards such as titles and positions to win over the majority of Scottish noblemen, the English administration manoeuvred the Scots Parliament into accepting the Act of Union in 1707; in effect, to vote itself out of existence.

Though Robert Burns was later to write a song with the bitter refrain 'We are bought and sold for English gold/Such a parcel of rogues in a nation', not every lord and landowner in Scotland succumbed. Thus Lord Belhaven was moved to point out:

> My heart bursts with indignation and grief at the triumph England will obtain today, over a fierce and warlike nation that has struggled to maintain its independence so long.

Familiarly known as Bonnie Prince Charlie, the Young Chevalier or the Young Pretender, Prince Charles Edward Stewart was born in Rome, and brought up for a military life. He came to Scotland only once, in 1745, to press the Jacobite claim to the British throne. Though some of the Scottish clans rallied to his cause, the last Jacobite rebellion ended in defeat at Culloden Moor in 1746. Later that year, the Prince escaped to France and remained in exile for the rest of his life. This portrait of him was painted by Antonio David.

In a sense, Scotland's history should stop with the Union of Parliaments in 1707, when Scotland's Parliament voted itself out of existence. However, 'North Britain' was to be the setting for further bloodshed as a Europe-wide power struggle was played out, which only ended on a sleet-swept moor near Inverness on a bleak April day in 1746.

The Jacobites and Prince Charles Edward Stewart

Even after the Union with England, the Jacobites remained an important political force on both sides of the border; indeed, they were an important element in European power politics, sheltered and encouraged, when it was politically advantageous, by France, Spain and Italy. Within a few years of the Union, dissatisfaction had become widespread in Scotland. Jacobite supporters seemed to have a narrow majority, especially in the Highlands. Though hardly impenetrable today, the Highlands at the time of the Union were still relatively unknown. Roads were poor or non-existent and cultural and linguistic differences meant that for many Scottish Lowlanders, and certainly for all English, the Highlands were simply an unknown country. The Jacobites continued to see the warlike clans, where every chief could call on his private army, as the best hope for advancing their cause.

Soon after King George I came to the throne, rebellion flared in the north. The key battle took place in 1715, at Sheriffmuir on the Ochil Hills beyond Stirling, where the Jacobites met a smaller government army led by the Duke of Argyll, head of Clan Campbell. The Highlanders' charge broke through on one flank, but was stopped on the other. Neither side could claim victory and the rebellion shortly petered out. James VIII (in Jacobite reckoning – he is otherwise known as The Old Pretender) landed in Scotland briefly after the rebellion was all but over, but hastily returned to France. It was left to James' son to prosecute the Jacobite cause, in possibly the most famous episode in Scottish history, the 1745 rebellion.

Romantic tradition has created in Bonnie Prince Charlie a tragic hero for all time. Many wistful songs of the 'Will Ye No' Come Back Again' variety commemorate 'The Young Chevalier' and his rash escapade in Scotland.

Charles Edward Louis Philip Casimir Stewart was born in Rome in 1720, and grew up imbued with the Stewart cause, thinking of himself from the first as a rightful future king. Certainly, he had the dangerous charm of the Stewarts in full measure and has often been portrayed as a captivating young romantic leading the Highland clans (representing a noble warrior race living in the past) in a futile and glorious escapade against the Hanoverian London-based government (symbolising Lowland oppression and hard-nosed commerce). Yet the Earl of Mar, who led the 1715 Jacobite rebellion, and Cameron of Locheil, active in the uprising of 1745, were both progressive, improving landlords, who developed their estates commercially. Thus although the Jacobites supported the 'traditional' style of monarchy they were not necessarily backward-looking. Instead, the Jacobite cause provided a natural focus for men who were disenchanted by the government of the time.

Charles' campaign in Scotland lasted less than two years and ended in total defeat. At first, though, he met with some spectacular successes; at one point his army penetrated as far south as Derby, causing panic in London. King George II was packed and ready to flee aboard the royal yacht, and historians have speculated ever since what might have happened if Charles had continued south. Yet the hoped-for help from France in the form of an invasion from the south never materialised, and the Jacobite army – short of cash and provisions and never well disciplined – began gradually to disintegrate. By late 1745, the clan chiefs who supported

Charles wanted to retreat for the winter, but Charles preferred to fight on, still trusting in French support. Thus, the scene was set for the final confrontation.

Culloden: the last battle

Charles made an ill-advised stand at Culloden Moor, east of Inverness, with perhaps less than 5,000 men. Facing him on this level open ground, an ideal shooting range for artillery, was ranged an army of 9,000. These were under the command of the Hanoverian general William, Duke of Cumberland, who was, ironically, Charles' distant cousin. Among Cumberland's forces were three regular regiments of Lowland Scots (which subsequently became the Royal Scots, the King's Own Scottish Borderers and the Border Regiment), the Royal Scots Fusiliers and also militia raised mainly from Clan Campbell – hence there were as many Scots fighting for the Government as fighting for the Prince. Charles' depleted, exhausted army was cut to pieces by superior firepower. That cold, wet April morning on a bare moor marked a turning point for the Highlands and was the last major battle fought on British soil.

It was here that the Duke of Cumberland earned his title of 'Butcher'. In the aftermath of the battle, the British Army subsequently committed what some say were the worst atrocities in its history. The wounded were bayoneted where they had fallen. Then the field was ringed by sentries for two days before execution squads were sent in to despatch any surviving Highlander. A widening wave of atrocities spread out from the battlefield in the aftermath of the slaughter, as the army exacted a terrible retribution from the local civilian population. Women and children, the families of nearby farmers among them, were casually butchered, irrespective of their sympathies, Jacobite or otherwise.

Jacobites were hunted down all over the Highlands (and Scots were even stoned or attacked in London!). Army patrols, with the tacit approval of Cumberland and other commanding officers, simply destroyed and looted every settlement in their path. Suspects were hanged, transported or imprisoned. It was the beginning of a campaign that would change the Highland way of life for ever. Feted in London, Cumberland had the flower 'sweet william' named after him; in Scotland, he is recalled by the weed 'stinking willie'. No British Army regiment today lists Culloden among its battle honours.

The Young Pretender had five months more in Scotland, sheltered by his supporters. It was during this time he was aided by Flora MacDonald, whose story is told in Part Two.

Charles was 'hot' property with a price of £30,000 on his head. (Not to be outdone, Charles offered £30 for the capture of King George!) The former sum was huge for the eighteenth century and yet while, for instance, the Prince's supporters could not get help to charter a boat out of Stornoway, nobody actually betrayed him. The Jacobites were later to boast that his magnetic charm ensured that he was protected wherever he

went. However, it seems more likely, given that only a small proportion of the clans actually came out for him, that his small band of loyal supporters kept him well away from the many spies and Government sympathisers who would gladly have turned him in. Legend and fact, Jacobite mythology and historical reality, have been confused ever since the Prince's Scottish escapade.

Culloden today is perhaps one of the most haunting places in Scotland, with an atmosphere curiously unaffected by the merry tinkle of tearoom and the chattering bus party. The Jacobite cause split families and communities. The National Trust for Scotland's visitor centre on the site, with its displays and audio-visual programme, does much to correct the myth that this was somehow a simple England versus Scotland conflict. In addition to the Scots fighting for the government army, many clansmen were expressly forbidden by their chiefs to fight at all. Perhaps they realised it would all end in oppression. Out of about 30,000 fighting clansmen in the Highlands, about 5,000 gave Charles their support, often only after their chief coerced them. Lord Lewis Gordon, third son of the Duke of Gordon, for instance, raised his regiment for its destruction at Culloden only after telling the men of Speyside that if they did not answer his call they would have their homes burned. It seems likely that those that did join him had their homes burned anyway when the British army passed that way *en route* for the battlefield.

There were no more Jacobite uprisings after Charles escaped to the Continent, never to return to Scotland. In response to this last rebellion, the government started work in 1748 on Fort George – a huge military fortification east of Inverness, controlling the approaches of the inner Moray Firth and linked by military roads to other forts in the Great Glen, running south-west from Inverness. Fort George survives today as one of the most complete eighteenth-century military works in Europe. It still has an army presence, though its guns have never fired in anger.

Along with the garrisons came the legislation: the banning of tartan and the wearing of arms; the forfeiture of Highland homelands belonging to Jacobite clans, as well as the stripping of all power from the chiefs. In the new order, many Highlanders turned to emigration, to seek work either in the industrial Lowlands or in the New World far beyond. Before the century had ended came the forced emigration – the brutal uprooting of the Highland Clearances.

 THREE

TOWARDS
THE MODERN AGE

By the eighteenth century, but before Culloden, the clan system had perhaps passed its peak: the power of the chief was by then not absolute and without regard to Lowland law and order. However, at least in some places, chiefs still kept expensive courts and prestigious retainers, and also applied their own justice. By this time many chiefs leased much of their lands to a network or hierarchy of 'tacksmen', who were sometimes related to the chief. They in turn rented land to other tenants who farmed it. Wealth was judged by cattle: hence cattle dealing and what was euphemistically termed cattle 'lifting' – which was really stealing or 'reiving' – was a way of life, and often a way of survival in hard winters. The tacksmen and the tenants together also formed an armed band or private army for the clan chief in times of war.

Meanwhile agricultural improvements were spreading from the Lowlands and beginning to have some effect at least in the more favoured parts of the Highlands. Some effort was also being made by the authorities to improve roads. Military roads, for example, were the result of the need to be able to move government armies around speedily to keep law and order. Even before Culloden, some Highlanders were supplementing their income working on road-building projects. Some of the chiefs were spending their own rents 'Lowland-style' on rich clothes and French wines. In short, Lowland market forces were beginning to make a slight impression on Highland tribal society. In its heyday, a common clan practice was to foster the children of chiefs with another family, usually that of a tacksman, as a kind of bonding with the rest of the clan. By the eighteenth century, some chiefs instead were sending their offspring to Lowland schools whence, no doubt, they returned suitably filled with the Lowland notion that their own background was barbarian. Besides, some of these 'educated' sons of chiefs took Lowland (or even English!) wives and had grand town houses in Edinburgh to maintain.

Following the breakdown of tribal Highland society in the post-Culloden upheaval, by the end of the eighteenth century about three-fifths of Highland landowners lived outside the Highlands. In the aftershock of the last Jacobite rebellion, the old values of the clans were rooted out by force of authority, and the powers of the old-style clan chieftains – some of whom were Jacobites and had had their estates forfeited

42

anyway – were swept aside by legislation. Some forward-looking High-land landholders, including those who had not come out on the losing side and had perhaps, through education and inclination, better standing in Lowland society, survived the post-Culloden purge to carry out their own improvements.

From Culloden to the Clearances

Modern Scotland would inevitably have crept into the Highlands with a subtle erosion of the old ways. Culloden simply accelerated the process. Suddenly, it seemed, cattle could be 'exported' safely to the Lowlands where a growing population needed to be fed and clothed. Very soon sheep, already grazing the border hills, were introduced to Highland pasture. Timber was another resource to be exploited – and some say it was Speyside timber workers fooling around with tree trunks who invented caber tossing by accident!

On the coast, fishing could also be productive, while the soap and glassmaking industries further south demanded the chemicals created by

Though Skye is best-known for the Cuillin Hills, other parts of this beautiful island also show dramatic landforms. The Quiraing is noted for the most spectacular example of landslipping in Britain – the edges of ancient lava-flows have broken away and slip imperceptibly towards the sea. Within the jumble of crags and pinnacles stolen cattle were formerly hidden.

43

drying and burning kelp (long brown strands of coarse seaweed, sometimes in Scots called 'tangle'). Some Highland chiefs, especially those with
islands or long shorelines in their landholdings, hoped to make their fortunes with this new industry. By 1784 the Highland and Agricultural Society was active and for a while it seemed that commerce and prosperity
might at last come to the Highlands. Just as in the Lowlands, new settlements were founded, such as Inveraray, created by the Duke of Argyll and
planned as early as 1740, or Ullapool, built by the British Fisheries Society
in 1788. The Grant family founded Grantown-on-Spey on Speyside and
there are many other Highland examples, including the highest village in
the Highlands, Tomintoul.

However, a 'Golden Age' of Highland prosperity simply did not happen. In the poor lands of the west there were no fortunes for all to be
made, though progressive landowners insisted that old methods of runrig
or strip cultivation should be abandoned for better methods of crop growing. As in the Lowlands, they tried to enclose and break in new ground.
Perhaps an inherent memory of security in landholding under the clan
system kept many of the tenants on diminishing parcels of land under the
new ways, where at least the introduced potato could sustain them. The
tacksmen, the former middlemen who no longer fitted in to the general
scheme, emigrated and took some of the tenants with them. This was the
situation noted by Johnson and Boswell in their tour of the Hebrides in
1773. Landowners did not at first encourage their going, needing man-
power for the kelp lifting. However, by the end of the century, despite
emigration, the limited agricultural improvements had actually increased
population. Some landowners had done well out of cattle, sheep, kelp or
fishing.

But things began to go wrong in the early nineteenth century. With the
ending of the Napoleonic Wars, the price of cattle fell. Besides, Highland
agriculture on poor acid ground could not really compete with that on
more favourable Lowland soils. Around the same time a number of chemical processes were developed as a substitute for kelp by-products, which
rendered its gathering and processing uneconomic. Even the herring
seemed to have swum away from once-favoured sea lochs, making fishing
more hazardous and uncertain than ever.

It is over-simplistic to state that Culloden turned the Highlands into a
desert. Certainly, the old tribal ways had gone forever. For a while, modern economic ways had been tried with varying degrees of success: even
taking into account the drift away to find work, in some places, at least, a
larger population than ever before was living off small parcels of land. But
by the early years of the nineteenth century, it seemed to an increasing
number of Highland landowners that in grim economic terms the best
way of maintaining their estates was by sheep farming.

The coming of sheep

People had to give way for sheep as early as 1785 when there was a large-scale clearance on the estate of MacDonell of Glengarry. In the 1790s, Ross-shire had known violence between the local folk and incoming Lowland shepherds. Ironically, soldiers from the recently built Fort George had marched to quell the disturbances. These were certainly far from isolated instances. Having taken a decision to put the land to sheep, many landowners' attitude to their tenants inevitably changed: the tenants' farming activities simply got in the way of efficient sheep rearing. Good portions of ground were needed for grazing instead of potatoes. On mountain pasture, traditionally where the Highlanders took their cattle, alpine-style, for the summer, there was competition between the tenants' cattle and the new flocks of sheep. Worse, the locals' own primitive wiry little sheep (as survive today in breeds such as the Soay) might interbreed with the new and precious Blackface or Cheviot. In short, the people had to make way for the new style of agriculture.

Highland Clearances

History has recorded that the most notorious of the 'improvers' was George Granville Leveson-Gower, second Marquess of Stafford, whose background was in coal and wool. An Englishman without a word of Gaelic, he was the richest man in Britain. As well as his vast estate in England, he had acquired much of the Scottish county of Sutherland by marriage in 1785 to Elizabeth Gordon, daughter of the last Earl of Sutherland. More than 5,000 people (some say nearer 10,000) were forced from their homes by their agents, irrespective of age or health, between 1807 and 1821. In a catalogue of brutality, the clearance of Strathnaver has perhaps become the most notorious in the memory of the Highlanders. Not only were the crude cottages of the occupants set ablaze, in many instances the occupants themselves were prevented from retrieving their own belongings. In some cases, old folk were still inside the dwellings when they were set alight. The principal factor of the estate, Patrick Sellar, was later brought to trial for arson and culpable homicide, only to be acquitted.

Yet it is to oversimplify the matter to label these wealthy landowners as despotic rulers. Many felt they were acting for the greater good, and invested in roads, bridges and harbours to generate prosperity. A few even tried to rehouse the tenants on marginal coastal land. It would also be wrong to suggest that the Clearances destroyed a life which was peaceful and idyllic. Food shortages were commonplace, dwellings of the ordinary folk were dark and damp, and they led a subsistence existence. However, the inherent brutality of displacing a population can hardly be excused or easily explained away.

Clearances, in one form or another, and with varying degrees of cruelty,

45

took place from Perthshire right up to Shetland. Today, far up Highland glens, the 'stravaiging' (wandering) visitor will still come across the tumbled walls of communities abandoned and all but reclaimed by turf and heather, and to this day sheep-nibbled. On high ground the outlines of summer sheilings can still be traced. These sad remnants of an infamous chapter in the Highland story date, depending on location, from as late as the 1850s. For example, on Skye, Lord MacDonald cleared Boreraig and Suishnish in 1853. Arguably the saddest of all the evidence is to be seen today in Croick Church in Glencalvie, Easter Ross. Scratched on a window pane in this little church are a few pathetic messages, dating from 1845 and written by the displaced local inhabitants. They record the days after the Laird of Kindeace sent out his factor to evict 90 people from the glen. The folk took shelter in the local churchyard. There they were witnessed (and interviewed) by no less a person than the editor of *The Times*, John Delane, who duly published a report. He saw infants in cradles, placed closest to the smoky fire, and, like the others, sheltering under poles and tarpaulins. What, in the end, happened to the glen's inhabitants after their eventual departure from the churchyard, history has not recorded.

Today's Highland cattle, wide-horned, shaggy and usually docile, are well-suited to the rigours of a cold Highland spring. The old-style cattle raised in the Highlands and taken south by drovers were actually much smaller, and black and wiry.

Workshop of the Western World

Though the focus of unrest was the Highlands and the greatest misfortunes occurred there, the rest of Scotland should not be overlooked. After all, most of the population lived there. In the latter half of the eighteenth and well on into the nineteenth century, the Lowlands made great strides forward in industrial output. The area around Falkirk is sometimes regarded as the cradle of the industrial revolution in Scotland. Local blast furnaces at nearby Carron used local coal together with local iron ore to manufacture pig-iron as early as 1759. A century later more than a quarter of Britain's output came from this area. In 1843, still two years before the dispossessed families shivered in the Glencalvie rain, a railway had linked Glasgow and Edinburgh for the first time. The Clyde meanwhile was channelled and deepened, enabling the growing shipyards on its banks to play their part in earning Glasgow and the Clyde the title of Workshop of the Western World.

The Clyde is not only associated with the romance of the much later Cunard liners – especially the *Queen Mary*, launched in 1934 – but also with an earlier generation of ocean greyhounds, the tea clippers. The most famous of these, the *Cutty Sark*, was launched from the Dumbarton yard of William Denny and Brothers in 1869. The last regular tea race to bring home the new season's crop was in 1872, after which competition from steamships going through the Suez Canal rendered these sailing vessels uneconomic. However, the *Cutty Sark* continued to earn her speedy reputation in the Australian wool trade, coming home to Britain in 69 days in 1887–8, when the average voyage time was 100 days. The *Cutty Sark* took its name from the scanty dress (literally short shirt) worn by Nannie, the most appealing of the witches in Robert Burns' poem 'Tam o' Shanter'. As many Scots can tell you, the poem's climax has a rapidly sobering-up Tam being chased by the witches. Nannie grabs at Tam's mare, Meg, just as they reach the keystone of the Brig o' Doon. The ship's figurehead shows Nannie stretching out her hand to grab at the mare's tail. Paradoxically, for a vessel with so many associations with Scotland (her designer was Hercules Linton from Inverbervie on the east coast), she is preserved in England at Greenwich, London.

However, though the Clyde's great days as a shipbuilding centre have now mostly gone, visitors to Dumbarton today can still see the Denny Ship Model Experiment Tank, a unique testing pool which was formerly used to evaluate hull designs. Thus, out of the heat of heavy industry, could come a peculiarly Scottish rivet-studded romance, an enduring image of Scotland far removed from misty glens and tartan warriors.

Not only was this enduring romance associated with floating craft. In Glasgow, by the end of the nineteenth century, the amalgamation of various firms to form the North British Locomotive Company created the second largest steam-engine builder in the world. The 'NB' sent its products across the globe: to the prairies of Canada, the pampas of Argentina, the hot deserts of Australia, as well as China, India, South Africa, Russia – in fact to just about anywhere it was possible to lay the iron road. Now, long after the last heavy hammer has been silenced and the last steam-chest bored out, even those workaday products have attained a special aura and nostalgia. Museum curators scour the world for Scottish-built industrial products. For example, Glasgow's Springburn Museum, on the site of the now-vanished loco building works, has re-imported an impressively large steam loco whose South African working life ended in the 1980s.

Another enduring legacy from Scotland's industrial heyday in the nineteenth century is the wealth of grand mansions and country houses which its industrialists, self-confident Victorian entrepreneurs, could afford to build. The Clyde may have been the waterway from which Scottish products went round the world, but at Helensburgh, the Rosneath Peninsula, Dunoon or Garelochhead, its waters lapped on shorelines placid and far removed from heavy industry. There, discreetly amid the woodlands, or boldly on the green hillslopes, still stand fine examples of mansions in the 'Scots baronial' style, pinnacled with turrets and fancy gables. Some are still in private hands, others are now hotels. Most have a story to tell: there stands the former home of an ironmaster; next door a textile manufacturer or a successful brewer. Some of these 'baronial' country house hotels still reveal the original owner's taste for wood panelling, richly carved, or an expensively marbled entrance hall. Scotland's Victorian legacy of fine buildings has a romance which owes much to the confident style of the successful entrepreneur both around the Clyde and far beyond.

The legacy of two particular entrepreneurs, however, survives not in stylish houses but in the surviving buildings in which they practised their unique brand of capitalism: the mills of New Lanark.

New Lanark: monument to Utopia

Scottish rivers formerly powered mills of various kinds, from humble flour mills serving local communities to larger textile mills. But only one river, at one point, achieved the combination of volume of water and speed of flow to power a textile project on a really grand scale: the river was the Clyde, and the place New Lanark.

The Clyde from Glasgow downstream can hardly be described as a placid and picturesque watercourse. However, upstream, the area which is today sometimes called Clyde Valley or Clydesdale, is very different. The waters flow by rounded hills, past farmlands and woods. Near the ancient market town of Lanark, still 32 km (20 miles) from Scotland's largest city, the Clyde tires of its winding gentleness and instead roars through a spectacular sandstone gorge and careers over waterfalls (in Scots known as 'linns'). Dense woodlands clothe the banks above white

water steaming into black pools. In 1783, an already successful Glasgow businessman, David Dale, brought the pioneer of industrial cotton-spinning, the Englishman Richard Arkwright, to this spot. He saw the potential of the site and so David Dale bought the ground and set to work. By the end of the century, New Lanark, as Dale called the development, had become the largest single industrial enterprise in Scotland. In 1793, over 1,100 employees tended these machines, of which over 800 were young boys and girls.

Dale was no tyrant. Hours were long but housing and educational facilities were, for their day, very good. Many of his child-workers were orphans, well cared for, while another source was Highland emigrants who had left their homeland for reasons described earlier in this chapter. Instead of the New World, they found work at New Lanark. (One of the streets to this day is called Caithness Row.)

This theme of philanthropy was further displayed by his later business partner and son-in-law, Robert Owen. This ambitious Welshman had strong ideas of equality and social welfare and saw this model village as an ideal place for his own social experiments. Eventually, to the mills and blocks of houses he added The New Institute for the Formation of Character and also Robert Owen's School, intending them to be the first steps in the creation of a society without crime, poverty or misery: the fundamentals of 'Owenism'. As the years went by, all of his efforts were directed towards worker and community care. That this enlightened system was operated in an out-of-the way valley in southern Scotland is one of the most fascinating aspects of New Lanark. Visitors came from all over the world to see this system of benign capitalism in operation. Owen later went to the USA to promote his ideals in the village of New Harmony in Indiana. The cotton trade continued down the decades under new owners, the principles of caring and education never quite drowned out by the clatter of mill machinery.

Eventually, the winds of economic change blowing throughout Scotland touched the community in the sheltered river valley. By the mid-twentieth century the mills and housing had fallen into decay, with only a tiny population. Today, thanks to the New Lanark Conservation Trust, much has been restored. Visitors can enjoy not only the spectacular scenery, but also a visitor centre with an audio-visual 'time trip', a working loom and all kinds of experiences to revive the past. Many of the buildings, skilfully converted, are occupied once more.

New Lanark's heyday was undoubtedly in the early nineteenth century. It is equally significant that perhaps the greatest monument to Scotland's industrial age, the Forth Rail Bridge, belongs to the nineteenth century, though much later. In fact, the country's high point as an industrial nation was over by the time of World War I. Local mineral resources were becoming harder to work, other nations were better placed geographically or were using more modern technology. Scotland's future seemed to lie in smaller-scale industries, better placed to maintain the reputation for quality which had been earned since the industrial revolution.

49

Joseph Walker, the founder of Walkers Shortbread Ltd, pictured outside his first bakery in Torphins in 1898, the year he started the business.

Quality Scotland

Looking at the Highlands' story, the greatest export from the north from 1750 onwards seems to have been people. It is their descendants who today form some of the Caledonian societies and clan associations stretching around the globe. Perhaps it was the emigrants' determination to create a better life, to be successful in facing new challenges, that contributed to the Scottish image of quality built up by the Scots overseas. The reputation for quality had certainly been demonstrated by the durability of materials in iron and steel, such as ships and railways. Perhaps the reputation had also been promoted, consciously or otherwise, by the Scots at home, robbed of their Scottish nationality, yet still seeking an identity which even the image of glorious tartan warriors, created by Sir Walter Scott, did not entirely satisfy.

Whatever the reason, Scotland has tried to make the most of its association with quality. Its malt whisky is a conspicuous example of promotion under this banner, involving small-scale production under the watchful eye of skilled and experienced individuals. Harris Tweed, which merits its own characteristic orb-shaped brand of authenticity, is still made by craftsmen in their own houses on looms producing only a 70 cm (28-inch) wide cloth. Genuine Shetland knitwear carries a similar hallmark of the skills of the individual. Even household names in food manufacture such as Macfish or Baxters, irrespective of their size, have the same characteristic of a touch of tradition, the input of a hand which relies on generations of hard-won experience, even if the hand is now aided by up-to-date technology. Another important feature is not only that many have stayed small or, even when scaled up, have retained the personal touch of a small concern, but that many are also to be found away from the 'central belt', the long established zone of heavy industry.

The story of Walkers

The River Spey is said to be the fastest flowing of Scottish rivers. It is famed for its salmon and, even today, for its pearls (the pearl mussel being a sure indicator of pure water). The Spey has cut a broad channel out of the Grampian mountain massif. Ancient ice-sheets long ago widened the river course – certainly enough for the area to justify the name of Strathspey (strath means a broad valley). Meltwaters from the last Ice Age also helped carve out river terraces or flats along the river. In modern times these level terraces between hillslope and running river have provided opportunities for both agriculture and settlement. Farms and villages prosper in the shelter of the high hills all around.

One of the most attractive Speyside communities was founded in its modern form in 1812 as a planned settlement by an improving landowner, Charles Grant of Wester Elchies. He gave the settlement the name of Charlestown of Aberlour, which is usually shortened to Aberlour, the original parish name where Aber signifies mouth or confluence – in this case the Lour burn. Aberlour today is neat and well kept, its solid granite houses fronting a main street of generous proportions typical of the early nineteenth-century planned community. Above and below the little place can be noted typical Speyside occupations: forestry and quality cattle breeding, as well as the intermittent plumes of steam marking the sites of malt whisky distilleries. But the main employer there is Walkers. The company plays its role in maintaining Scotland's reputation for quality, in fact the pure and simple ingredients from which its shortbread is made have helped make it the most successful exporter of shortbread in Scotland. A string of awards have acknowledged the Walkers' recipe for success in modern Scotland: start with a quality setting, use the very best of produce and maintain the skills of the craft – in this case the master baker – to produce a consistently high standard of finished product.

In 1909, the firm's founder, Joseph Walker, already an experienced baker, moved his little business from Torphins (near Banchory in Aberdeenshire) to Aberlour. There he was joined by his two sons Joseph and James. This was the Edwardian heyday of the sporting estate. Speyside, already favoured by climate and setting, had further advantages, among them a loop of the Great North of Scotland Railway running

both to Keith and hence Aberdeen and the south, as well as to the Highland Railway at Boat of Garten for Aviemore. This line then led over the
highest railway pass in Scotland (Drumochter, 453 m/1,485 ft) to Perth
and beyond. It was these rail connections which helped transport the aristocrats and industrialists, even the king himself, for the shooting season
on Speyside. The railway also helped in the despatch of orders from the
soon thriving bakery, which certainly did extra business when the local
grand houses, famous for their lavish entertaining, were occupied with
shooting parties. Thus in addition to the local year-round customers, traditional bakers like Walkers were encouraged in their craft by the
demands of the sporting visitors. With a commodity which was relatively
transportable and non-perishable like shortbread, the well-to-do also
spread the word about its quality to their contacts in the south.

As the years went by, the Walkers' business prospered. The motor van
also played its part in meeting customer needs. (The first acquisition was a
Model T-Ford van in 1923.) By the mid-1930s, not only day-to-day loaves
and biscuits were doing well: there was also an impressive demand for
shortbread and cakes. Clearly the Walkers insistence on only the finest
flour, butter and other natural commodities, had already created an
impression. By the time of World War II, shortbread was packaged in tins,
making it even more transportable. The post-war era saw gradual expansion through the 1950s and 1960s, with a trebling of the workforce in the
10 years to 1973. In spite of a difficult economic climate for Scotland in the
1970s, which saw major (but less high quality) bakers dramatically
rationalise, Walkers single-mindedly refused to compromise on its high
quality ingredients. Expansion in the 1970s continued, with a move to
new custom-built premises.

Walkers pure butter shortbread maintained its world leader position in
the 1980s, a market fact confirmed by the granting of the Queen's Award
for export achievement in 1984 and again in 1988. This is the highest
award given to British exporters and it is very rare for a bakery to receive it
twice. Europe has also recognised the company's achievements, with
Monde Selection in Geneva awarding Gold Medals for Walkers' products
in 1986 and again in 1989.

Just as important was another milestone: the first ever Highland Business Award went to Walkers in 1987. This award is granted only to the
company making the greatest contribution to the economy of the Highlands of Scotland. As history shows, the Highlands have had their share of
troubles. That they are beautiful and inspiring is beyond doubt, but scenic
qualities and job opportunities do not necessarily go hand in hand.

Tourism has undoubtedly played its part in Speyside. Distillery visiting,
walking the Speyside Way or observing the home life of the osprey are
just a very few of the pastimes which have now been added to the game,
fishing and shooting which still attract visitors for the season. This emphasis on tourism has undoubtedly benefited Walkers, supplying its products
not only to quality hotels but also gift shops and a range of outlets catering
for the discerning visitor. If a quality image brings visitors to Scotland in

the first place, then Walkers plays its part in the pattern of excellence as a modern business dedicated to maintaining high standards. The company uses local skills handed down over the years – the third generation of Walkers are now in the business – and firmly blends this past experience with a modern outlook, while all the time being true to first principles of never compromising on quality.

The blending of the traditional and the modern to achieve unbeatable quality can certainly be appreciated in the taste of the product, but Walkers bridges past and present in other ways. The distinctive packaging features the tartan of the Grant family, founders of Aberlour. This clan anticipated the modern convention of allowing the clan chief to ordain the clan's tartan. Before the Jacobite rising of 1715 (which the Grants did not support) Sir Ludovick Grant of Grant ordered his men to wear a particular and distinct red tartan. Later family portraits suggest that not all his dependants did so, and simply went on wearing the 'setts' (designs) which appealed to them, as it seems most other Highlanders did before Culloden. However, when the Grant tartan was composed a century later, Sir Ludovick's original instruction was followed, lending a particularly authentic and historic flavour to the pattern. (The Grants were one of the Anglo-Norman clans, perhaps originally from Nottinghamshire. Their name is from the French *grand*, meaning big. Sir Lawrence Le Grand, the first named ancestor, is recorded as Sheriff of Inverness in 1258.)

As well as the use of authentic Grant tartan, Walkers' products recall other historical links. Their logo of a Highlander stooping to kiss a lady's hand does not simply represent the essence of giving and receiving. It is a representation of Prince Charles Edward Stewart and his meeting with Flora MacDonald during the manhunt after the last Jacobite rebellion. Her 10-day dangerous escapade with Charles, told in Part Two, was only one episode in an adventurous life. Other historical figures recalled on Walkers' packaging include Major General Sir Ewan John Murray MacGregor of MacGregor, nineteenth Chief of the Clan Gregor. This distinguished chief, much loved and respected in his time (1785–1841), served with distinction in India, receiving terrible injuries while storming a Mahratta fort in 1818 – a reminder of the important role of Highland regiments in Britain's imperial wars. MacGregor also took a leading part in the pageantry surrounding King George IV's notable visit to Scotland in 1822.

However, a chief is not the only MacGregor recalled in this way. Helen MacGregor, wife of the famous folk-hero Rob Roy MacGregor, is also portrayed. She represents the Highlands as they were viewed in the popular literature of Sir Walter Scott's time. The true-life Rob Roy, whose life is recalled in Part Two, was the subject of a novel by Scott in which Rob's real wife, Mary of Comar, became fictionalised as Helen – an impressive female warrior, a kind of tartan Amazon, capable of leading the clan against the Lowland authorities!

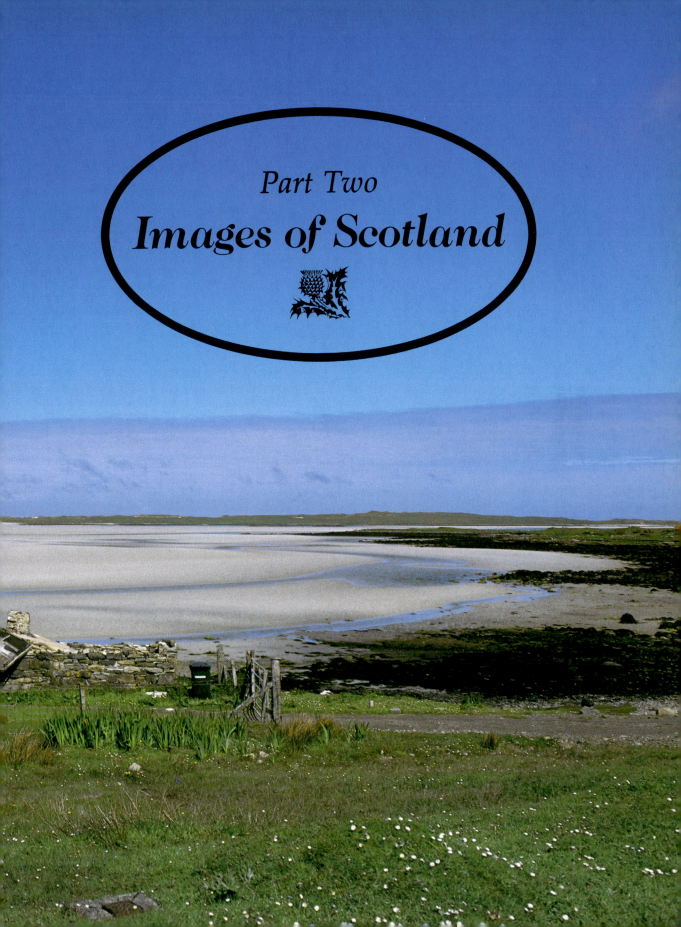

Part Two
Images of Scotland

 FOUR

SCOTLAND'S HIGHLAND HERITAGE

The Government Act of 1746 (19 Geo.II,c.39) was uncompromising:

> '. . . no Man or Boy, within that Part of Great Britain called Scotland, other than such as shall be employed as Officers and Soldiers in His Majesty's Forces, shall, on any Pretence whatsoever, wear or put on the Clothes commonly called Highland Clothes (that is to say) the Plaid, Philabeg, or little Kilt, Trowse, Shoulder Belts, or any Part whatsoever of what peculiarly belongs to the Highland Garb; and that no Tartan, or party- coloured Plaid or Stuff shall be used for Great Coats, or for Upper Coats.'

The edict goes on to warn of penalties of jail or transportation. It was just one of a series of government statutes meant to destroy the clans forever.

In 1822, King George IV visited Edinburgh. The previous notable royal visitor had been the bloody Cumberland (King George IV was his great-nephew) and his intention had been, as related earlier, to destroy 'tartan terrorism' forever, aided by legislation like that quoted above. Yet when the king attended a levee at the Palace of Holyroodhouse he was clad, to the amazement of many who were present, in a magnificent Highland costume (though to maintain royal modesty he wore silk flesh-coloured pantaloons to hide his legs).

The tartan

Thus in 76 years the utter defeat of Gaeldom seemed to have been turned to a victory. The barbarous cloth of a minority culture in 'North Britain' had received royal approval. Besides the tartan rig of the king, the new breed of Highland masters who had flocked to Edinburgh to dance attendance on the royal presence were likewise strutting around in magnificent costumes, some with eagles' feathers of chieftains in their new bonnets. Tartan had become wildly popular and fashionable, and society clamoured for the latest and best patterns.

 What is tartan? For a humble folk fabric it has raised extraordinary controversy, with two opposing camps. One group tends to debunk the

mythology with which tartan is now surrounded, for example the partly spurious heraldry linking clan and cloth. The other side delivers a counter-argument to demonstrate tartan's antiquity. Both groups snipe at each other from time to time in newspaper columns and in tartan guides and histories. The visitor can be forgiven for being confused by contradictory evidence. Only one clear fact emerges: in modern Scotland, tartan is fully exploited as a potential symbol of the nation, with a wide range of uses.

Some say the first mention of tartan is in the Exchequer Roles of the Lord Treasurer in 1538, where there is an order for a roll of cloth of 'Heland Tartane', the material intended for 'hoiss to the Kingis Grace'. This sounds very much like a pair of tartan breeks (trousers) for King James V. The debunkers point out that 'Heland' simply refers to the cut of the finished garment and that the word is really 'tiretane' which was a kind of material of French origin. All very mysterious, especially as tartan is an English (or Scots) word anyway – the word for the striped cloth in Gaelic has always been *breacan*. If there is no agreement on its very name, perhaps there is accord in the statement that the pattern is at least truly Scottish? Unfortunately not. Cloth looking suspiciously like tartan turns up in fifteenth-century works from the Italian school of painting in Siena. Japanese prints of the eighteenth and nineteenth centuries also show distinct tartan checks in clothing. The argument claimed by the 'anti-kilters' is that it is a natural way to weave cloth of different colours.

In the days before modern aniline dyes (which use a coal tar-derived chemical to help make them colourfast), the manufacture of cloth using natural products as dyes was a basic concern of Highland communities. Fleeces were sorted then scoured (cleaned). Then they were dried, teased out, oiled and combed, enabling the wool strands to be wound on bobbins. The wool could then be spun to the desired thickness and dyed before being woven. The cloth was scoured again and afterwards 'waulked' which meant rolling, kneading and generally thumping it until it had been shrunk and felted. This was a communal occupation of the womenfolk, hence the rhythmic, repetitive Gaelic waulking songs sung to make the task less tedious, which are part of Scottish musical tradition. As for the colours produced, these naturally depended on which dye stuffs were available locally. In early times fir-club moss was used as a mordant, that is, a chemical which fixes the colour permanently on the wool. Other substances, especially stale urine, were used to darken the dyes. From early times some dye stuffs had been imported, notably indigo, but even in the Highlands the range of colours was surprisingly extensive: blues and greys from plants such as bilberry (Scots 'blaeberry') or the roots of yellow flag iris; reds from blackthorn or ladies bedstraw, among others; purple from bramble, elder, etc., and notably from crotal – lichens in variety; yellow from bog myrtle, birch leaves and bracken root; browns from a number of tree species and also lichens; black from alder, water lilies, nettles, and so on.

This was the literally homespun cloth which clad the Highlander. Not that he reached into the wardrobe to buckle on the smart little kilt seen

Pages 54–5: Now mostly rebuilt or abandoned, traditional black houses in the Western Isles, such as this one on North Uist, were snug, if smoky. The thatched roof and the rounded corners of the walls offered less wind resistance. One black house has been preserved by Historic Scotland at Arnol, on Lewis.

57

today. The Gaels, according to some authorities, had always worn loose garments, usually described as a long shirt or tunic. Trews (trousers), also sometimes worn in the Highlands, seemed to be a link with the type of dress worn by the inhabitants of Scotland before the Scots arrived. Trews later became tartan in the Highlands, having survived in parallel with shirts and other loose garb – after all, in their non-tartan variety, trews of all kinds are still the standard garb of the Lowlanders today! By the seventeenth century the long skirt was displaced by a blanket-like dress known as a belted plaid. At least, that is one version of events – other authorities claim the plaid is much earlier. (Perhaps it depended on the weather: the Highlander was unlikely to be smothering himself in a hairy blanket in the middle of a heatwave.)

The usual dimensions given to the tartan plaid are 1.8 × 5.5m (2 × 6 yds). It served as both camouflage by day and bedding by night. To dress, the owner put a belt on the ground, pleated the material lengthwise over it, lay down on it and gathered the material round both sides, buckling the belt round his waist. This resulted in a skirt of pleated material below and a voluminous armful above. This could be flung over the shoulder, formed in a hood or left hanging. On this point most authorities at least agree. However, opinions soon diverge on the evolution of this tartan

blanket (that is, the plaid or great kilt or *feilidh-mor*) into the *feilidh-beg* (philabeg or little kilt) which is the apparel worn by men today. Traditionalists are understandably uncomfortable with the story that suggests the modern kilt was invented by an Englishman! He was one Thomas Rawlinson, who was involved in the first half of the eighteenth century with iron-working in the Lochaber area (presumably using local timber to fire the smelters). Noticing that his Highland workers were encumbered by the upper part of the plaid, he experimentally cut off the top part, leaving the skirt-like pleated garment seen today. Finding it comfortable he often wore it himself, thereby creating the tradition, still seen widely in the Highlands to this day, of a non-native incomer enthusiastically adopting Highland costume!

Tartan and the army

Plaid, kilt, jacket and trews all seem to have been around at the time of Culloden. Yet the kilt did not vanish with the ban on tartan. The British government quickly realised that to channel the warlike Highlanders into fighting for the 'right' side would create an unbeatable fighting force. The Campbell militia had demonstrated this at Culloden, and Highland companies had been raised from at least as early as the beginning of the eighteenth century. The Black Watch or 42nd Regiment was only one of a number of Highland regiments raised to fight for the British government's cause. From 1757, it battled against the French in America. The English General James Wolfe, a young officer at Culloden, took the Fraser's Highlanders up the Heights of Quebec in the Canadian campaign. The Gordon Highlanders were raised to fight in India. The fighting Highland regiment has been a martial image cherished by the British nation down through the wars of the empire and through both world wars to the present day.

This martial spirit was at least partly embodied in uniform. Tartan was thus preserved and encouraged by the military. Highland dress was modified according to the needs of the wearer: ceremonial, social or on campaign. This adoption as regimental garb partly explains the evolution of some of the paraphernalia of today's Highland wear. For example, the sporran started as a totally practical leather pouch made of supple, hard-wearing deerskin with two drawstrings, one to open and one to close the bag. In early times it was not even worn in front but more usually found attached to a belt. Metal clasped varieties seem to be one offshoot from the simple pouch. The military embellishments turned it into the narrow-mouthed, grotesquely be-tasselled and hairy creation of more modern times. Some authorities even quote the example of a grand chief whose sporran was not only ornate but also had a secret pistol as part of its mechanism – the pistol going off if the sporran was opened incorrectly!

As for other aspects of Highland dress, the light deerskin shoes of the Highlander on the hill became heavy brogues, while the little knife used for skinning and other purposes became the modern *sgian dhu*, suitably

Opposite: *The Ceremony of the Jedhart Callant (the callant is the leading man, always a bachelor) is just one part of the annual celebrations at Jedburgh, in the Scottish Borders. Rideouts, cavalcades, gymkhanas, concerts and dancing also feature prominently. As a good example of the way that tartan has been adopted throughout Scotland as its own potent symbol, the festivities inevitably also involve a pipe band in Highland dress, even if the Borders seem a long way from the Highlands.*

encrusted with decoration and usually translated as black knife. However, there is even an uncertainty with this simple dirk, which modern Highland dress requires to be kept tucked out of sight in the top of the sock or hose. The black element in the name may not have anything to do with colour but could be translated as hidden, that is, a weapon kept out of sight. In fact, the word black in this context may be linked to another controversy: whether or not the regiment called the Black Watch was named after the colour of its tartan or whether black described its main activities. It was raised specifically to police the Highlands and prevent cattle stealing. Many cattle owners paid a rent to bands of Highlanders in a kind of protection racket known as blackmail – black meal, that is, hidden payment – or rent. The Black Watch, or perhaps 'hidden watch', was formed to stamp out this practice.

It would be misleading to suggest that tartan survived exclusively because of the role of the army. The laws banning its wear were repealed in 1782 but even when they had been enforced they had been regularly flouted, particularly by wealthy families, as surviving contemporary portraits show. However, the repeal at least brought tartan back in the news and caused a revival of interest, though less among the poor tenantry scraping a living from their potato patch than from the fashion conscious of Scotland and England. This is not, of course, the only time that military uniform has proved to be a source of inspiration to the fashion industry.

The tartan image

The role of the Highland regiments during the Napoleonic Wars continued to bestow a certain romance and heroism upon the tartan. Meanwhile, the narrow order of neo-classicism, which saw nature as something to be tamed and restrained, was crumbling before a new feeling in art and literature that we now call Romanticism. Sufficient time had elapsed since they were a threat to order for the savages in 'North Britain' to seem imbued with a certain unspoiled charm. English Romantic poets such as Wordsworth and Coleridge visited accessible parts of the Highlands as part of the cult of the picturesque which developed as an offshoot at this time. Simultaneously, the sentimental songs of Lady Nairne, the daughter of a Jacobite laird, had become very much to the public's taste. Sir Walter Scott's romantic fiction reinforced these changing attitudes; crowds had flocked to the Trossachs which he had peopled with knights and heroines in *The Lady of the Lake* in 1810. Finally, 'North Britain' was to become wholly acceptable with the visit of King George IV in 1822.

This event was central to the rehabilitation process. Sir Walter Scott was appointed to organise the royal visit and ensure its success. He called upon the lairds and chiefs to declare their loyalty by parading before the King with a tenantry dressed like the clansmen of old. He marshalled the growing interest in the Highlands, already manifesting itself in clubs and societies patronised by wealthy landowning families. Landowners like Lord and Lady Stafford, stung by criticism of their harsh usage of their

tenantry during the Highland Clearances, responded enthusiastically. The Staffords kitted out a body of men for the grand parade in Edinburgh, no doubt by coercion, in the same way as they had already raised three regiments of the Sutherland Highlanders to fight the French and the Americans. Other chiefs did the same, among them Alastair Ranaldson Macdonell of Glengarry, one of the most touchy and flamboyant of the new-style Highland chiefs. In his time, he had squabbled with the company building the Caledonian Canal through his land, fought a pistol duel, gone about with a retinue of servants like an old-style chief and, in short, was an idiosyncratic anachronism and founder of the Society of True Highlanders. He was also the inventor of the Highland cap known as the Glengarry bonnet. Such chiefs were the vanguard of the tartan conquest of Edinburgh during the royal visit, when the tartan warriors were the sensation of the day. This sealed the fate of the kilt which was thereafter destined to be Scotland's national dress.

Tailors and manufacturers rushed to supply orders. The most famous name amongst these manufacturers was Wilsons of Bannockburn. It was already a major weaving company at the time of the king's visit but, in spite of opening a new 40-loom weaving shed, the business could not keep up with the demand which the event generated. Wilsons was well accustomed to designing tartan almost willy-nilly to the public's taste and certainly was not the only company engaged in this activity. Not only Scottish manufacturers were involved; weaving companies as far afield as Norwich in England competed for the lucrative trade. By the early years of the nineteenth century an export market had developed, supplying some unlikely places – even slaves in Barbados were dressed in Scottish cloth, as were several of the natives of Rio de Janeiro, if contemporary order books are to be believed. In these order books are several letters asking for the latest and brightest pattern books. This makes tartan sound like a wall-paper or fabric collection and is a far cry from the vexed question of the authenticity of clan tartans.

This is the most emotive area in the tartan debate. The 'anti-kilters' claim that almost all the patterns were re-invented under commercial pressures when tartan became fashionable. The traditionalists point to evidence suggesting that locally available dye stuffs meant that tartan cloth could be readily identified with the specific areas of its origin. One of the historic texts which support this is *A Description of the Western Islands of Scotland* by Martin Martin in 1703. He notes how

> Every Isle differs from each other in their fancy of making Plads as to the stripes, in breadth and colours. This humour is as different through the mainland of the Highlands, in-so-far as that they who have seen those plads, are able, at the first view of a man's plad, to guess the place of his residence.

From such evidence it is only a small step to identifying tartan with a specific clan. Nevertheless, at Culloden, supporters of the Prince wore white cockades (ribbons folded into flower shapes) in their bonnets to

An incident in the Scottish Rebellion, 1745 was painted by a Swiss artist, David Morier, commissioned by the Duke of Cumberland to paint a series of pictures of British regiments. Here, Barrell's Regiment is attacked by the Jacobite forces. Eight discernible Highlanders are wearing at least 23 different tartans and this has been used as evidence that the association of clans with specific tartans is a fairly modern one. Morier used real prisoners as his models and was noted for his accuracy.

distinguish them from the Hanoverians. They could not be identified by tartan alone.

Whatever the truth of the matter, some pre-Culloden tartans do certainly exist and can be seen in collections today, for example at the Scottish Tartans Museum at Comrie in Perthshire or the West Highland Museum in Fort William. Though modern aniline dyes are widely used in tartan manufacturing today, it is also possible to see old-style vegetable dyes being used in small-scale tartan manufacture. This can be found at the Highland Tryst Museum at Crieff in Perthshire where a local weaver makes tartan on a hand loom. (An old-style sporran maker can be seen at work there as well!)

In conclusion, it can be seen that the army maintained a tartan tradition. The cloth then became steeped in romanticism and by a superb propaganda exercise was projected as a Scottish symbol, particularly at the time of the 1822 royal visit. In turn, the play-acting and dressing up in fantastical costumes appealed to a wider and wider number of Scots at home and abroad, even though some Scots were uncomfortable with it. Robert Louis Stevenson, a loyal enthusiast of all things Scottish, later described the process as 'the ghastly romancing of Scotland's scenery and manners'. Long before that, the *Scotsman* newspaper on the 28th July 1830 had printed a satirical poem which made the point that most of the 'Highlanders' appearing at fashionable parades and levees were not even from the Highlands. Commenting on a parade at Bruntsfield in Edinburgh a certain 'Alister Macintrowsers' laments:

Oh never since then within me
Did feelings of poetry rise
Till the Highlanders at Bruntsfield
Filled my soul with surprise –
With shame and grief to think of
The tartans and the hose,
The Gaelic tongue and the bagpipes
Turned into raree shows . . .

To think of such sham Highlanders
Sinking our great renown
To a raree show at Bruntsfield –
Their charge for't – half a crown.

Nevertheless, in spite of such reservations on the purloining of this shadow of Gaelic culture, the tartan image was embraced wholeheartedly. The building of Balmoral Castle by Prince Albert and Queen Victoria, with its wall-to-wall tartan carpets, wallpaper and furnishings, further provoked an outbreak of 'tartanitis' which has continued down to the present day. Thus the kingdom of the Gael, rooted out and mostly scattered to the four corners of the earth, had a curious triumph in the end, with its native cloth becoming a potent symbol of all Scotland. To the majority of Scots in the Lowlands it probably came about in the nick of time. The culture of the Gael may have been a closed book to many, but at least it was known to be vigorous and to have a poetic spirit or romance which *sassunachs* (Lowlanders) lacked. Besides, in the early nineteenth century most of Scotland seemed on the point of absorption into a larger British community. To many Scots, in the midst of their identity confusion – perhaps busy trying to cast off their Scots tongue, or make their way forward in commerce and industry – it may have seemed that all that Lowland Scotland could offer to distinguish it from England was its formal institutions such as the Law or the Church. Neither of these was really colourful enough for the stuff of romance.

Thus Scotland, shorn of its nationhood yet knowing it was somehow not simply a part of England, in casting around for a new identity found the tartan and all it represented. It was the ideal badge of identity to proclaim Scotland's differences, its traditions, and its quality of essential Scottishness. The tartan's function as a rallying point and symbol of quality is in the end more significant than any squabble over the authenticity of any one particular check or hue. The evolution of tartan is a fascinating tale, but its role today as a powerful national symbol is probably more important than ever.

The clan

In Gaelic the word *clann* means children or descendants. The chief of the clan was a kind of tribal father to whom lesser chieftains, tenants and sub-tenants all owed allegiance. They would take up arms at his request and fight to avenge a wrongdoing, mount a cattle raid or settle a territorial dispute. The chief's 'right' to his lands went back further than written laws, while the clansfolk were linked by blood and belief with a common ancestor. The clan system and the tribes within it gradually evolved out of early Scottish history with Pict and Scot, Norse and Norman all playing a part. As noted in Chapter One, Anglo-Norman adventurers came north and many married into Celtic society, some even into the ancient earldoms. Pictish territories were gradually infiltrated by settlers, who were encouraged by the Scots monarchy; and the introduction of the feudal system during the eleventh century defined the northern boundaries of Lowland rule. Pictish elements retreated into the mountains and Scot and Norse intermarried. The result of all this was – eventually – a clan system operating more or less independently of the Crown by the thirteenth century.

Norman elements can be noted in clans such as Fraser, whose name is ultimately linked to French *la fraise* – referring to the strawberry-shaped device on their shields – or Bruce, from Brix in Normandy. A Norse link is found with the Clan Macleod, descended from Leod or Liot, son of Olaf the Black, the Norse King of Man. Liot's two sons, Tormod and Torquil, founded the two main branches of the clan. Meanwhile, Somerled, a twelfth-century warlord descended from Irish royalty, married the King of Man's daughter. His eldest son, Dougall (dark foreigner in Gaelic), became the founder of the Macdougalls, while Somerled's second son is claimed to be the founder of Clan Donald and other clans.

As for Pictish links, some say the Gunns, a clan from the far north of Scotland, are descended from Pictish tribes pushed out by the new settlers. Also, some historians think that when the rebellious Picts of Morayshire were finally cleared to make way for Anglo-Normans, they crossed the Moray Firth and settled in the mountain fastnesses of Caithness, where the Mackays were soon strong, thus giving this clan at least a possible connection with the Picts. Pictish elements turn up in MacNaughton as well, from Nechtan, a name used by Pictish kings. One other feature is the frequent association of clan names with religious denominations: Macnab means 'son of an abbot'; Buchanan 'son of the canon's house'; Mactaggart 'son of a priest'; Macpherson 'son of a parson' and so on. Clearly the early Celtic clergy were not celibate!

With the main Scottish power base lying to the south, the clans were able to develop in relative isolation, to form alliances or make enemies amongst themselves as the ambition of the chief, the success of the harvest, or even the severity of the winter dictated. Clansfolk lived a life more or less of self-sufficiency, and the wealth of the clan was counted in cattle.

Not surprisingly, stealing cattle was endemic – not simply as a way of life, but often as a way of survival, for many occupied a harsh landscape.

Communication, especially the call to arms, was a special problem in mountainous terrain. It is sometimes overlooked, in their strong association with ben and glen, that many of the clans of the west, particularly the Clan Donald, were skilled sailors. Great oared galleys or *birlinn* were used to get around the islands in the summer months. On land, swift runners were part of the chief's retinue. Given that the humblest tenant felt himself tied by blood to the chief, any call to defend the chief was answered immediately. This summons often took the form of a fiery cross, which consisted of two burning sticks tied together by a bloodstained strip of cloth. It was carried round the clan lands by a team of runners and an immediate response was expected. After battle formation had been joined, the clansmen used their slogan or battle cry to identify themselves in whatever action they were involved, especially in the confusion of, for example, a night raid or a mass attack. (Slogan itself is said to be a Gaelic word from *sluagh* – army, *gairm* – cry.)

But there was more to the clan than a group of barbaric warrior-herdsmen squabbling with their neighbours. An important member of the chief's court was the bard, who was both the poet and recorder of the clan's story. He could relate lineage and also compose an epic poem describing a heroic feat by a clansman in battle. The chief also had a piper, another hereditary post. The music of the chief's house at an earlier stage would have been played on the clarsach (a type of small harp), but by the seventeenth century the bagpipe with its more war-like tones had replaced the clarsach's peaceful and plaintive strings. Clearly, a taste for higher decibels had developed by the late Middle Ages, or perhaps it was simply more difficult for a chief to coerce his men to follow into the thick of a fight if they were led by a sturdy clansman thinly plinking on a small harp. Instead, the bagpipes or warpipe of the Gael could be heard from a considerable distance over the din of battle and could even communicate messages to rally or advance. There are even instances of pipers captured by enemy clans having their fingers cut off as a precautionary measure. At least one piper who was tried after Culloden said in his defence at his trial in York, England, that his was a musical instrument and that he was otherwise unarmed in the battle. The authorities decreed that the bagpipe was a weapon of war and hanged him. The pipes were then banned.

Scotland's most famous piping family was the MacCrimmons, who lived on Skye and were hereditary pipers to the MacLeods. One Donald Mor MacCrimmon is credited with developing the set-piece of theme and variations which became known as pibroch (Gael: *piobaireachd*) in the early seventeenth century. Later, six generations of the family were to teach in their college of piping at Borreraig. Their method was oral (as was so much of Celtic tradition) using a complicated system of mouthed sounds called in Gaelic *caintearachd* (chanting).

The traditional instrument of the Highlands, which all of Scotland embraced partly because of the 1822 visit of King George IV, is in its

constituent parts not unique to Scotland. Using a reed as the basis for a musical instrument is widespread, while a bladder used as an air reservoir seems to have been developed by other cultures in mountainous areas in Europe. However, the Highlanders developed it further than any other group.

Bodyguards and bards, pipers and dancers all had a part in the retinue of the chief, particularly if he went visiting for prestige purposes. In fact, there is evidence that in the clan heyday the grandest of chiefs went around accompanied by his very own Highland Games.

Highland Games

These have strong echoes of old clan ways and have become one of the most colourful traditions associated with 'tartanry' in Scotland, with games and gatherings taking place throughout the summer. Some say that they originated with the chiefs as a method of choosing the best bodyguards and the fittest of fighting men. However, not all of the chief's requirements were warlike. Musicians, dancers and entertainers were important for prestige and could also find a place in a chief's household. Competitions were the best way of selecting staff and supporters: champion runners made good couriers; strongest men trusty bodyguards; and athletes could be matched in contest with those of rival chieftains.

Perhaps games and gatherings were once the way to celebrate special events like weddings or a chief's initiation. However, the people of the village of Ceres, actually in Lowland Fife, claim the oldest event; they maintain that a gathering was held to celebrate the safe return of the village's bowmen after the Battle of Bannockburn in 1314, and that an annual gathering has taken place ever since. By way of counter-claim, the eleventh-century King Malcolm Canmore is said to have been the first Scottish monarch to hold a gathering at Braemar. He organised a race up Craig Coinnich, near the present village, to choose a new courier.

Opposite: Though this is at Grantown-on-Spey, caber tossing can be seen at any of the Highland Games in the summer season. This most characteristic of Highland tests of strength is said to have originated on Speyside, when Highland lumberjacks amused themselves by flinging large logs around!

In the dancing at today's Highland Games many ancient elements can be seen. The Romans reported that the ancient Caledonians danced wildly round their swords; some historians say that the linking and weaving movements and clockwise directions in Scottish country dancing betray Celtic origins, indicating an early sun worship ritual; while the circle of the reel is symbolic of the circle of life! Another aspect of the development of Highland Games is the part played by the Highland regiments in upholding traditions. As well as developing and modifying Highland dress and tartan after Culloden, they kept alive the spirit of the games.

Many events at 'modern' Highland Games still have an affinity with ancient clan custom. One particular characteristic in the tests is the use made of equipment still related to everyday items which once would have been found close at hand. Strength could be measured by simple means, such as the lifting or throwing of stones. In the Highlands such a stone was

known as *Clach Cuid Fir*, meaning Manhood Stone. Sometimes the weighty item was kept close by a chieftain's castle, perhaps for entertainment or testing visitors. There is a well known example outside the churchyard at Balquhidder, north of Callander (the burial place of Rob Roy), and the notable Stones of Dee are at the Bridge of Potarch on Deeside.

From struggling to lift giant stones, it is only a short step towards throwing them, hence 'putting the shot'. This Highland fling would originally have used large rounded stones, easily found in river beds. Such a stone became a *clach neart* – stone of strength – and weighed about 14 kg (30 lb); the hammer used in hammer-throwing would have been an everyday implement. However, the use of natural materials is best seen in tossing the caber, probably the best known event. The caber (usually pronounced kay-ber) has hardly changed since earliest times. It is a long, straight tree-trunk of native Scots Pine, shorn of all branches, which tests strength, agility, co-ordination and balance. The competitor first props the caber upright, thick end higher. He then lifts the end of the caber into his cupped hands, supporting it with a shoulder, and starts making a run, balancing the caber at the same time. At the right spot, he stops and hoists the caber into the air, for it to turn over cleanly and fall in a '12 o'clock' position. No two cabers are the same and each Games has its own caber. The world-famous Braemar caber is 6 m (19 ft 9 in) long and weighs 60 kg (132 lb).

In addition to the events described above, Highland Games usually include tugs-of-war, hill races, and other athletic events like pole-vaulting. But they are unique because they also combine sport with music and dancing, so Highland dancing and piping competitions may also take place, as well as non-competitive parades and march-pasts by pipe bands.

Officers returning from the army after the Battle of Waterloo prompted the first modern Braemar Gathering, perhaps the most famous Highland Gathering. Its continued popularity was assured when Queen Victoria fell in love with Deeside and built Balmoral Castle. The Royal Family became regular patrons of the Braemar Gathering from 1848 onwards. Though Braemar is perhaps the most famous Games, Cowal (near Dunoon in Argyll) claims to be the largest with its famous 'March of 1,000 Pipers'.

These are just some aspects of tartan and clans. Certainly, if modern tartans are exploited fully as a favourite symbol of Scotland, then modern Highland Games are also wildly popular with visitors. Likewise in this transformed culture of the Gael, modern clan associations are powerful bodies, in the sense of their being able to bring together people from all over the world who somehow feel a sense of kinship with each other. About 250 years ago, the clans who rose in rebellion were broken with no thought for their culture or way of life. Contemporary opinion, as expressed by Lowland Scot or English alike, simply saw the process of suppression as one of civilising a primitive culture. Yet the heritage of the tribal society which once existed in the Highlands has spread around the world, and retains deeply felt links with the original traditions of the Highland society that was so ruthlessly uprooted.

FIVE

SPEAKING SCOTS

Some outsiders think all Scots sound alike, partly because the media have perpetrated the myth that all the inhabitants of Scotland speak with the distinctive tones of the guttural Glaswegian. Yet anyone listening with an attentive ear will soon discover that this is not the case; just as it becomes easy to taste the difference between an eastern malt whisky and an island malt, so it is just as simple, with practice, to tell an Aberdonian from a native of the Hebrides.

Some native Scots can go further and locate a dialect to a very small area: farming and fishing communities still sound different to each other in rural Buchan, even within the narrow category of the particularly authentic form of Scots still spoken in that windy corner of north-east Scotland. In fact, Scotland offers a diversity of language, and a wealth of vocabulary not found in English, as well as a number of constructions or idioms using 'English' words in a Scots way. But how did the tongues used in Scotland today – Gaelic, Scots and English – come to sound different from the dialect of England's Thames Valley which, because of the nearness of this area to England's capital, became elevated to 'standard English'?

The origins of Scots and Gaelic

Far back in time, before even the Scots came to Scotland, the language spoken was probably a kind of Welsh: the P-Celtic mentioned in Chapter One. Echoes of this early language survive in place names such as Aberdeen or Aberdour, as well as the characteristically Scottish prefix 'Pit-' meaning piece (of land, or farm) as in Pitgair, Pitsligo, Pittodrie, Pitfour and dozens more. When the Scots came from Ireland in the fifth century they brought with them their Q-Celtic or Gaelic which replaced the earlier form. By about the tenth century Gaelic was spoken all over Scotland except in the south-east. Place-name evidence includes the use of 'Inver' instead of 'Aber' (both meaning mouth or confluence) as in Inverness, Inverurie, Inverewe and so on.

Early Scots

The south-east part of Scotland was, in a way, the starting point for the Scots language as we know it today. It came within the sway of a Northumbrian kingdom ruled by Angle and Saxon tribes which had settled from Europe. The Angles gave their name to England while the Saxons are recalled in the Gaelic word *sassunach*, meaning Saxon, Southerner or Lowlander. One example of early written evidence of this northern Anglo-Saxon language, established by the fifth century, is the few lines from the poem 'The Dream of the Rood' inscribed on the eighth-century Ruthwell Cross (badly damaged in 1640, sadly), which can be seen today inside Ruthwell Parish Church, east of Dumfries.

It was this northern form of Anglo-Saxon which was to become Scots. It was strongly influenced by a Norse element (which gave kirk for church, muckle for much, breeks for breeches, and many more). Its expansion was aided by the Scottish King Malcolm marrying an English wife, Queen Margaret. The Norman Conquest ultimately brought a new wave of settlers north. Though many were French-speaking Normans, others spoke the northern form of English. By the twelfth and thirteenth centuries there was certainly a linguistic mixture, with Gaelic in retreat northwards and westwards. Early French words which came in around this time include 'provost' (Scots for mayor), 'vennel' (lane) and 'baillie' (burgh official). Gaelic, even in retreat, certainly influenced this northern form of speech, whose speakers readily adopted the old-established place-name features: hence glen and ben, loch and bog.

As the centuries passed, Scotland's French links continued to be evidenced by later borrowings: 'cowp' (to overturn); 'tassie' (cup); 'grosset' (gooseberry). Sixteenth-century imports included 'fash', as in 'dinna fash yerself' (do not become upset), as well as caddy, 'jalouse' (deduce) and even, it has been suggested, Hogmanay. At around the same time, Scotland's contact with other parts of Europe was also influencing vocabulary. From the Dutch we have golf, and a host of (to non-Scots) less familiar words: for example, 'redd' as in 'redd-up' (tidy), 'mows' as in 'nae mows' (uncanny), 'plot' as in 'plottin' (overheated), and dozens more. This language, increased in vigour by its borrowings and in widespread use by the thirteenth/fourteenth centuries, was called for a time 'Inglis', to distinguish it from southern forms of English. In 1494 there is the earliest reference to it as Scots or 'Scottis'. It was the language of court, of literature and of numerous translations. Its finest flowering was between the mid-fifteenth and mid-sixteenth centuries, with some linguists noting it as having the same relationship to English as Danish has to Swedish or even Dutch to German.

The spread of English

In the sixteenth century, with the events of the Reformation, the Scots language began to be eroded. Scotland was aligned with England in religious matters: literary English was introduced into Scots homes through printed versions of the Bible, translated from Latin. The King James Bible was printed in English, not Scots, and with the spread of this and other printed works in English, Scots became increasingly confined to everyday domestic use, with English as the dominant literary medium.

Another blow to Scots as a language was the departure of King James VI to his London court in 1603. Scots was no longer spoken at court, as it ceased to be the language of the king. Then came the disappearance of the Scots Parliament in 1707, when English became the official language of administration. The loss of religious status after the Reformation, court status after 1603 and political status after 1707 combined to spell the end of Scots as a full-scale all-purpose medium.

The Gaelic language still survives in the Western Isles or Outer Hebrides, as here in Ersary on Barra, not only as the vehicle of traditional song and story, but also as the everyday speech of the local folk.

71

The development of Gaelic

Meanwhile, how had Gaelic developed? Irish and Scots Gaelic had begun to diverge in the thirteenth century, though the first printed book in Gaelic – a translation of John Knox's *Liturgy* (1567), by Bishop Carsewell – used a form of classical Irish. (Carsewell's home was Carnasserie Castle, today a scheduled monument, on the A816, 14 km/9 miles north of Lochgilphead.)

In the heyday of the Lords of the Isles (the medieval warlords who ruled in the Highlands), Scots Gaelic probably was at its full artistic height. Gaelic poets, for example, held pride of place in Gaelic society and were encouraged under patronage to take the lead in intellectual matters. However, after the power of the Lords of the Isles was broken, Lowland control of matters military and political in the Highlands inevitably spread the language of the *sassunach*.

Even so, there was still a strong poetic and oral tradition in Gaelic. Poets flourished in the sixteenth to eighteenth centuries. (At Dalmally a signpost points to a monument erected in memory of Duncan Ban McIntyre (1724–1812), sometimes called the Burns of the Highlands; from the monument there is one of the very finest views in the Highlands, looking over Loch Awe to Ben Cruachan). The eighteenth-century poet Alexander MacDonald or Alasdair MacMhaighstil Alasdair was not only a nature and love poet, and author of many defiant Jacobite rants, but also the creator of what has been described as the greatest sea poem written in Britain, 'The Birlinn [Galley] of Clan Ranald'. It brilliantly displays the power of the Gaelic language and celebrates the values of its culture. Yet it is hardly a well known work, such are the difficulties of capturing the spirit of the original in translation, though one of Scotland's greatest twentieth-century poets, Hugh MacDiarmid, has perhaps come closest to achieving this.

Significantly, Alexander MacDonald was also a schoolmaster and wrote a Gaelic–English Glossary (1741) to aid the teaching of English in the Gaelic homelands. It is often commented that the folk of the Gaelic west speak the best English. By the time the Glossary was published, Scots was certainly not taught because of its low status. The Gael, learning the new language, moved straight from his or her native tongue to English, in a standard form shorn of 'Scotticisms' and pronounced with the appealing lilt which is still so distinctive today.

72

Modern Scots: the Scottish dilemma

From the eighteenth century almost to the present, the erosion of Scots as a spoken tongue has continued. Ever since James Boswell was thrilled when Doctor Samuel Johnson complimented him on his lack of a Scottish accent, generations of schoolmasters until very recent times have attempted to coerce the Scottish schoolchildren into aping 'standard English' in order to 'get on in life'. In the eighteenth century, respectable academics made up lists of 'Scotticisms' to be avoided. Elocution teachers in those days were in huge demand. It is even said that one such teacher's peculiar intonation was responsible for introducing the instantly recognisable 'Morningside vowel'. (Morningside is a district in Edinburgh said to be frequented by a particular type of well-bred old lady who specialises in this accent!)

However, Scots hung on in popular culture – in songs and ballads – and was bolstered to some extent by Scots poets, particularly Robert Burns. Yet even he represents the Scottish language dilemma. At his best, he effortlessly modulated from Scots to English; at his worst he created uncomfortably English drawing-room sentiments for the approval of the Edinburgh literary set. So great did the linguistic trauma become that until very recent times a Scottish schoolchild could win prizes for reciting Burns' Scottish verse, yet be punished for using the same words in class. Even Sir Walter Scott, so often described as Scotland's champion, only allowed Scots to be spoken between the characters in his books who represented 'the lower orders'.

In the meantime Gaelic, the Highland Clearances notwithstanding, appeared to fare better. It still proved a sound vehicle for prose and poetry (contrasting with Scots, which has no standardised spelling for written material – though the publication of recent dictionaries and a thesaurus will be useful here). The formation of An Comunn Gaidhealach in the 1870s, an association dedicated to preserving and encouraging the Gaelic language, also helped staunch the inevitable flow towards English. Scots had no equivalent until 1972, when a body known as the Scots Language Society was formed, although the poet Hugh MacDiarmid in the 1920s hoped for a full restoration of the Scots language and, in the 1940s, a generation of other poets such as Robert Garioch and Sydney Goodsir Smith began to show how Scots could still be used as a literary medium.

Gaelic has one further advantage. Because it is unlike English, it can to some extent borrow from it on occasion without necessarily weakening itself. This contrasts with Scots, which is easily confused and corrupted by English. Yet Gaelic certainly still suffers the setbacks of a minority language. As recently as 1981 the Western Isles MP's bill to promote Gaelic in the Highlands on roadsigns, in official documents and in other ways was thrown out by a London parliament. The 1980s also saw the loss of three Gaelic dialects: Appin, Aberdeenshire and Cowal Gaelic.

Revival

Since then, however, a number of hopeful signs have emerged, with our growing appreciation of heritage and 'popular' traditions in all walks of life. Gaelic playgroups are now undertaking the vital task of teaching children their native language. Comhairle na Gaidhlig was set up as a new organisation with responsibility for language promotion, leaving An Comunn Gaidhealach to the arts and the organising of the National Mod (the annual competition and artistic focus of Gaeldom). Gaelic teaching in schools and a Gaelic TV service are now realities. Despite earlier gloomy forecasts, the future of Gaelic seems brighter now than for several decades.

As for Scots, contemporary writers such as Billy Kay, particularly in his book *Scots: The Mither Tongue*, demonstrate the linguistic heritage which had been suppressed for generations. On publication, the *Concise Scots Dictionary* became a Scottish best seller for Aberdeen University Press. Far from being dead, Scots appears in all kinds of places; good Scots can still be heard in the theatre as well as on the factory floor. Thus, in spite of social and educational pressures, Scots survives in a variety of forms, weak and strong. As a visitor you can hear it by the quayside and the farmsteading, in shops, playgrounds and pubs: in some places modified

The beautiful scenery of Deeside captivated Queen Victoria and she spent as much time as possible at her beloved Balmoral Castle. In her time, there were still some Gaelic speakers in this part of the eastern Grampians near the Linn o' Dee. Gaelic in 'upper' Aberdeenshire clung on as recently as the 1980s, though very rare.

(because the speakers know you might want to join in), in others gloriously unrestrained. Some Scots are even waking up to the fact that they have within their grasp a whole vocabulary which has stood the test of time, a supplementary 'word-horde' denied to English speakers. Scots are even retrieving these words, long ago consigned to the attic of childhood memories, dusting them down like a wide-ranging verbal antique collection and trying them out in everyday contexts. Many are surprised to find how useful and resilient these words are.

Thus, as a visitor, do not hesitate if your host offers to see you the length of the station, as he is only offering to escort you to your train; or if a Scot asks where you stay, for the Scots often say this when the English would use live. Perhaps, if you are in self-catering accommodation, a Scots neighbour will ask if you need any messages – this is just an offer to do any shopping for you. These examples are just a reminder that on many occasions Scots use different constructions with words found also in standard English. Listen also for Scots vocabulary in everyday use: a 'dreich' day is dull and grey; a visitor 'sweirt tae gang hame' is reluctant to leave you; a job advert for an 'orraman' is one for a spare farmhand; and if the baby dribbles you can always give it 'a dicht with a daidlie' (a wipe with its bib).

The Scots even have phrases for those who spurn their own speech and prefer 'English'. The resultant style, often over-refined and affected, is colourfully called 'pan loaf'. This came about because a pan loaf was usually more expensive than a plain loaf! Meanwhile, the sound of an aspiring English speaker is described as 'bool in the mou' – a wonderfully deflating phrase literally meaning marbles in the mouth. Hardly a dead language!

 SIX

A MISCELLANY
OF FAMOUS SCOTS

Scotland's story is that of its people, especially those who were powerful, warlike or influential, and who by accident or design shaped events in this small nation: Wallace, who dared to stand against the armoured strength of England; Bruce, who secured the kingdom for almost four centuries; Mary, Queen of Scots, enigmatic and romantic; Prince Charles Edward Stewart (though born in Rome), the last of the Stewarts to unleash that dynasty's dangerous and persuasive charm to any lasting effect. There are other important figures: a handful of powerful regents; dukes able to pull strings; churchmen with the fire of conviction; and military leaders with the ability to inspire. There are still others recalled in tales and songs: border 'reivers' (rustlers) who met a bloody end; enterprising merchants who built grand castles; and ordinary folk who by accident achieved a lasting fame. Perhaps the best example in the latter category is Flora MacDonald.

Flora MacDonald

The everlasting appeal of Flora MacDonald is probably due to her 'ordinariness' – she was a down-to-earth Highland girl who, after persuasion, did as she was asked out of sympathy for a fugitive and did not expect reward. Thus, almost by accident, she played her role in an episode which became one of the most romantic in Scotland's story.

Fionnghal (Flora) MacDonald (1722–90) was born on the island of South Uist. At the time of her adventure with Prince Charles in 1746, she worked for Lady Clanranald, wife of the chief. Because of her Jacobite sympathies Lady Clanranald and, through her, Flora had been kept closely informed of the Prince's whereabouts after the Culloden disaster. Many writers have pointed out that Flora was not necessarily a Jacobite, but simply had a sympathy for the unfortunate state of the Prince. In fact, because of the great danger to her family, she was reluctant to aid the cause and had to be persuaded to play her part – particularly as her stepfather, Hugh MacDonald of Armadale in Skye, was in charge of the militia who were supposed to be hunting for the Prince.

76

By June the Prince was in the Western Isles and, after a series of narrow escapes around the coast, finally made another landfall in South Uist. Guided by a local schoolteacher called Neil MacEachain, the Prince and an Irishman called O'Neill who had been with him on the campaign travelled over moorland to Ormaclett on the west side of the island. Here they found a simple sheiling, used by the locals when they grazed their cattle in summer, where Flora MacDonald was awaiting them. The plan was to disguise the Prince as 'Betty Burke', a female servant, and conduct him to Skye to the home of Flora's mother and stepfather.

The preparations took six days to accomplish and the party left by boat just as militia landed nearby. MacEachain was posing as a manservant and the Prince was dressed in a calico gown, a quilted petticoat and all necessary female paraphernalia to hide his face and figure. The story is often told that Charles wanted to hide a pistol under his petticoat but Flora objected on the grounds that if he were searched the pistol would give him away. The Prince replied, 'Indeed, Miss, if we shall happen with any that will go so narrowly to work in searching me as what you mean, they will certainly discover me at any rate.' This remark says much for the Prince's sense of humour in time of great stress!

The party first attempted to land at Vaternish on Skye but were fired on by a party of militia. They later got ashore safely on a beach north of Kilbride. Leaving the Prince sitting on a clothes trunk on the beach, Flora went to Monkstadt House nearby, the home of the chief of the Skye MacDonalds. He had come out not for the Jacobites but for the government, though his wife, Lady Margaret, was a Jacobite sympathiser. However, when Flora arrived the moment was extremely awkward as Lady Margaret was entertaining some of her husband's militia friends. Flora remained cool enough not only to maintain an air of innocence but somehow to communicate to Lady Margaret the nearness of the Prince. Lady Margaret organised her kinsman MacDonald of Kingsburgh to take the Prince to Kingsburgh House for safety.

From this house, Flora and MacEachain went on ahead to an inn in Portree, with the Prince eventually following under cover of darkness that same evening. He left as 'Betty Burke' but dispensed with the disguise for the last time in a nearby wood, putting on Highland dress again. At the Portree inn, after a meal, there was a final parting: 'for all that has happened, madam, we shall meet again in St James's yet' Charles is reputed to have said, but he and Flora were not destined to meet again. A boat took him to Raasay and his life as a fugitive continued until he left the mainland in September.

Shortly afterwards, Flora was taken prisoner. She spent some months on a ship of war, then was taken to London in 1747 and confined for about two years. Fortunately, she was never ill-treated, and her reputation as a romantic figure developed quickly. Even in 1747 when confined in London, she was much feted as a gallant and faithful heroine and was even introduced to the Prince of Wales. She had her portrait painted by fashionable artists of the day and married the son of MacDonald of

Kingsburgh in 1750. Yet so much popular attention had no bad effect on her whatsoever. Dr Samuel Johnson, along with Boswell, met her in Skye in 1773. He remarked that her name would be forever 'mentioned in history and, if courage and fidelity be virtues, mentioned with honour'.

One year after she entertained Dr Johnson, Flora emigrated with her husband to North Carolina. In 1776, in the War of Independence, he became a Brigadier General on the Royalist side. He was made prisoner and Flora returned to Scotland in 1779. Eventually her husband returned to join her and they settled once more at Kingsburgh. She died in Skye in 1790 and her grave can be seen today not far from the place where she first landed with the Prince.

By the time George W. Joy (1844–1925) painted his version of Charles and Flora, the Jacobite cause was without any political or military threat and was instead the inspiration for sentimental songs and romantic portraits.

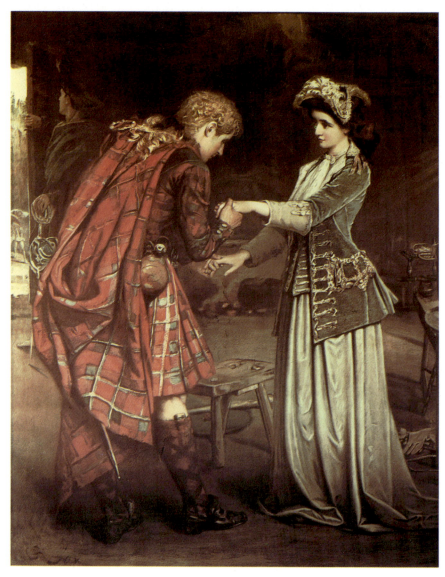

Rob Roy MacGregor

Other figures in Scotland's story are well known simply because of their romantic appeal. A good example is Rob Roy MacGregor (1671–1734), who became a 'legend in his own lifetime' – a kind of Scottish Robin Hood to whom all kinds of tales of daring were attributed. Some of them were even true!

Like Robin Hood, Rob Roy was popular with the tenantry because, even when hard-pressed by the authorities, there seems to have been much robbing of the rich to pay the poor. His story is particularly notable because, in a way, he was an anachronism – a clansman of old who lived out of reach of Lowland justice, surviving in a hostile environment through his courage and resourcefulness.

The life of Rob Roy

Rob was born in 1671 in Glen Gyle at the west end of Loch Katrine in the Trossachs, on a main cattle-droving road from the west. (The house, though private, can still be seen today.) He grew up in the cattle business, both legitimate and less so. Eventually he helped operate a 'watch', providing security guards for other people's cattle if they paid protection money. Through several adventures in recovering stolen cattle and lifting some for himself, he became a skilled swordsman and an expert in hillcraft.

Rob married Mary of Comar (Helen Mary MacGregor from a farm near Glen Arklet) in 1693. The 1690s were notorious in Scotland's history for the severity of the winters and it became increasingly necessary for Highlanders to raid cattle simply in order to survive. This practice was rife along the Highland edge, the territory of the MacGregors, because they could quickly descend to the rich pickings of the Lowland grazings.

In the first decade of the eighteenth century, Rob's business activities continued to prove profitable in legal cattle-dealing, almost-legal protection and, to Lowland eyes, quite illegal cattle-stealing. (As a Jacobite, Rob tended to lift the cattle of wealthy Lowland opponents of the Jacobite cause.) The Duke of Montrose made a deal with him to buy cattle for fattening and resale and some say that as much as £1,000 changed hands for the initial purchase. In mysterious circumstances, Rob's chief drover, MacDonald, then absconded with these funds. In a move that has been questioned by historians ever since, the Duke had Rob declared an outlaw and then, without giving him a chance to repay the money, burned his house and seized his lands. Was the Duke simply acting through greed and a desire to amass lands? Was it political? The Duke was against the Jacobites and perhaps suspected Rob of Jacobite plotting.

Whatever the reason, from 1713 to 1720 Rob lived outside the law. He swore revenge on the Grahams, the family of the Duke of Montrose, and quickly organised a network of sympathisers. He raided Montrose's cattle and even collected rent from his tenants, usually just ahead of Montrose's factor, the unfortunate Grahame of Killearn, who repeatedly seems to have borne the brunt of Rob's activities. MacGregor's men apparently always gave a signed receipt for any monies acquired in this way, in case the tenantry were accused of hiding the money themselves to avoid rent payment! Many tales of his exploits come from this stage in Rob's career. For example, one of Montrose's tenants in the village of Balfron was about to be evicted for arrears of rent. Having heard about this, Rob arrived ahead of the factor and left money with the tenant to clear off all debts. On his way to Stirling with the money, the factor was ambushed by Rob's men who thereby got the funds back.

Rob took part in the 1715 Jacobite rebellion and shortly afterwards came so close to capture that he actually put himself under the protection of the Duke of Argyll, head of the Campbells. Rob had Campbell blood on his mother's side but, in addition, so complex were the politics of the time that although the Duke of Argyll had commanded the government armies against the Jacobites, Argyll was also a bitter political opponent of Montrose. To this day, deep within Campbell territory in Glen Shira behind Inveraray, there is a 'Rob Roy's house'.

Rob was in fact captured three times, though he escaped each time. The first time, bound to one of Montrose's men while under escort to Stirling Castle, he persuaded the man to loosen his bindings and then dropped into the river as the company crossed the Forth. The second time he managed to escape from Logierait Castle where the Duke of Atholl had treacherously lured him; his third escape was from a company of soldiers in a narrow, overgrown part of the road by Loch Lubnaig, *en route* for Stirling Castle. It seemed that not even the might of the Hanoverian army could hold Rob.

Rob took part in the abortive rising in Glen Sheil in 1719 but by 1725 seems to have made his peace with the authorities. In that year a formal pardon was arranged by no less a person than General Wade. Rob resumed his cattle-dealing activities and died peacefully at his home in Balquhidder, on the edge of the Trossachs, in 1734.

Part of Rob's fame came because he was written about during his own lifetime. Even the king enjoyed his adventures – in spite of their political differences. A place in Scotland's folk memory became almost inevitable after Sir Walter Scott wrote the novel *Rob Roy*, which made him a symbol of a vanishing way of life in the Highlands – after all, Rob died only 12 years before the Battle of Culloden. From Scott's novel a play was derived which was very popular in the early part of the nineteenth century; it was even staged for King George IV on the famous 1822 visit to Edinburgh.

Sir Walter Scott

Sir Walter Scott (1771–1832) was born in College Wynd, Edinburgh. His chosen career was law but it is as a prolific writer that he is remembered; indeed, he was one of Britain's first best-selling novelists. His works are usually Scottish in setting and character, yet are considered a major contribution to English literature.

As part of the Romantic literary movement in Britain (the English poets Wordsworth and Coleridge were his near contemporaries), Scott promoted a new image of Scotland as a place full of Highland wildness and the vanished romance of the clans. This way of looking at the nation shaped outsiders' expectations of Scotland in a manner which still, to some extent, survives today.

The life of Scott

Scott's father was an Edinburgh lawyer and his mother a daughter of the Professor of Medicine in Edinburgh University. While very young, Scott was sent to his grandfather's farm near Smailholm to recover from illness, and it was here he first heard stirring tales of Border history. In 1792, after studying law, he became an advocate. As early as 1794 he was an enthusiastic member of the Royal Edinburgh Volunteers, a yeomanry regiment formed by those whose beliefs were shaken by the French Revolution and the fear of reform and upheaval in Scotland. In 1797 he married Margaret Charlotte Charpentier, daughter of a French refugee. He was appointed Sheriff of Selkirkshire in 1799. By 1805 his romantic poem *The Lay of the Last Minstrel* brought him fame and it was followed by other popular romantic works in verse.

In 1814 he turned to novel writing with the publication – at first anonymously – of *Waverley*. This was a huge success and all of literary Scotland buzzed with speculation as to who the author might be. Already well known as a poet, Scott later acknowledged his authorship of the book and his career as a popular novelist seemed unstoppable. *Waverley* is the story of a young English officer caught up in the 1745 Jacobite rebellion. The portrait of such central figures as the clan chief Fergus Mac-Ivor coloured readers' ideas of clan society for decades afterwards. (Many critics believe that Scott's inspiration for Mac-Ivor was Alastair Ranaldson Macdonell of Glengarry, one of the most enthusiastic supporters of the king's 1822 visit to Edinburgh, and a landowner who consciously modelled his lifestyle on the old-style chiefs.)

In 1826, Ballantyne's publishing business, of which Scott was a partner, went bankrupt and he was forced to write copiously to clear off debts. His wife died in the same year. By 1831 Scott's own health was failing; he went on a continental tour in hopes of regaining his health but died on 21st September 1832.

81

Scott preferred country to town life and had the country lover's sense of order and place in society, and also an abhorrence of the evils of the city. He was alarmed by the growing tide of radicalism and of the social reform demanded by weavers and other working groups; instead he used his works to hark back to what he believed was an ideal age, preferring to create a heroic image and a kind of Highland warrior culture. Nowadays Sir Walter is sometimes criticised for his stand against radical elements in Scotland. His lameness (as a result of his childhood illness) prevented him from any real military action but he was an enthusiast for playing at soldiers in the volunteer regiments formed to defend the old order against possible revolution. In Edinburgh, his mounted troop on one occasion fired against protesting miners and he also threatened rebellious weavers with his sabre. Scott was thus firmly on the side of the establishment.

His novels have stood the test of time better than his verse-narratives, though many modern critics point out that in dialogue passages he tends to use English for his heroes and aristocratic characters, reserving Scots for 'the lower orders'. Some see this as a disservice to Scottish writing – ironically, as the most realistic and vigorous dialect passages are usually in Scots! It could be argued, however, that Scott was only reflecting current attitudes to the Scots tongue.

Scott's home, Abbotsford, still stands on the banks of the River Tweed near Melrose. The original farmhouse was demolished to make way for this great storehouse of Scottish history, filled with relics and mementoes collected by Scott. A great number of artefacts such as Bonnie Prince Charlie's 'quaich' (drinking bowl), Rob Roy's broadsword, Bonnie Dundee's (Graham of Claverhouse) pistol, as well as a variety of other weaponry and relics of the past, are on display. The mansion includes an armoury, 9,000-volume library, entrance porch copied from Linlithgow Palace, library ceiling plaster-casts from Rosslyn Chapel, and a screen wall in the form of Melrose Abbey cloisters. Little has changed since Scott's day: his writing desk, chair and many personal effects are still there.

Scott wanted to be a poet and instead is remembered as a novelist. He did not attain the premier place in Scotland's poetic hall of fame. Instead that is held by an Ayrshire man, Robert Burns, who is undoubtedly one of Scotland's most famous sons, if only because he is the only figure, historic or literary, to be remembered in Scotland and elsewhere by an annual celebration of the simplest, most sincere but most enjoyable kind: the Burns Supper.

Robert Burns

Robert Burns (1759–96) was the son of a farmer who had moved to Ayrshire from Kincardineshire. Though he is often described as a 'ploughman poet', in reality he was fairly well educated for the times. His greatest contribution to serious literature was as a shrewd and satirical observer of his fellow man and his foibles. He is perhaps best remembered for his sentimental and lyrical pieces, which cannot be separated from the romance of his own humble beginnings. He also collected, arranged and amended many of Scotland's traditional folk songs. Probably the most important theme which runs through much of his work was his belief in the universal brotherhood of man:

> Then let us pray that come it may
> As come it will for aa that,
> That Sense and Worth, oer aa the earth
> Shall bear the gree, for aa that   come off best
> For aa that, and aa that,
> It's comin yet for aa that,
> That Man to Man the warld oer
> Shall brothers be for aa that.

Song: 'For aa That and aa That'

The life of Burns

His father, William Burnes (the spelling was changed in Burns' time), acquired land in Alloway, just south of Ayr, and built on it the small cottage in which the poet was born. The young Robert Burns' education had a literary flavour, through both his early teacher and his own inclinations. The tales, ballads and songs of Betty Davidson, an old woman who lived with the family, were an early influence, as were the works of Allan Ramsay, an earlier and less well known Scots poet. By 1774, Burns was working on his father's farm (then Mount Oliphant near Alloway) and had for the first time committed 'the sin of rhyme'.

By 1780 he had founded the Tarbolton Bachelors' Club for 'diversion to relieve the wearied man worn down with the necessary labours of life'. In 1781 he trained as a flax-dresser (or heckler) in the heckling shop in Irvine. It burned down in 1782. Worn out by the struggles of farming, Burns' father died in 1784 and, together with his brother Gilbert, the soon-to-be-famous poet rented another farm, Mossgiel. Around this time he began 'to be known in the neighbourhood as a maker of rhymes'. In 1785, his mother's servant-girl Betty Paton gave birth to his daughter, and in this same year he also met Jean Armour, later to be his wife. Out of poverty, passion and despair was born a major period of poetic productivity, with poems such as 'The Address to a Mouse', 'Holy Willie's Prayer' and 'The Cotter's Saturday Night' among many others.

This creativity continued into 1786, with much of the output published in the famous Kilmarnock edition, *Poems, Chiefly in the Scottish Dialect*. Jean Armour's father, discovering that his daughter was pregnant by Burns, served a writ on the poet, who did penance for fornication by being harangued in the local kirk! Jean produced twins and Burns planned to emigrate – though 'the feelings of a father' eventually prevailed and he

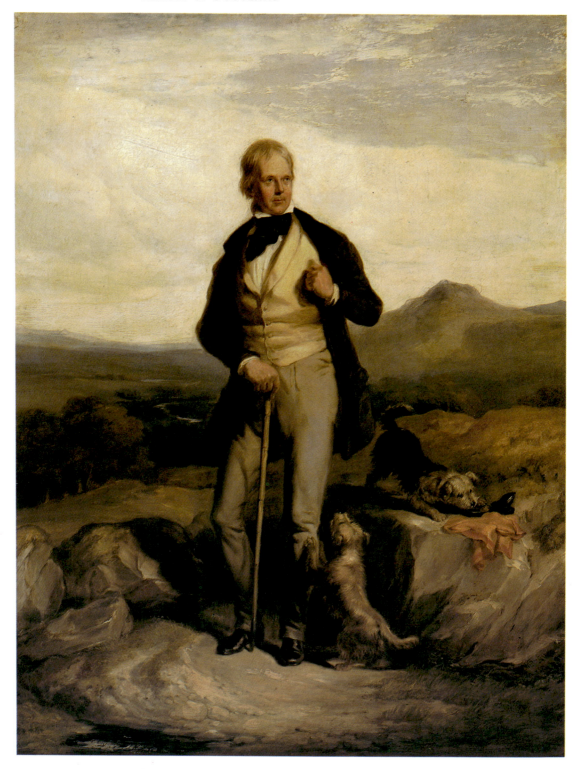

cancelled his passage to Jamaica. During this time he also managed a romantic interlude with Mary Campbell (Highland Mary), a shadowy figure in the Burns story, who died shortly afterwards. Whether or not Burns' entanglements at this period were more complex than those of any other handsome but penniless young farmer, in an age when rural life was straightforward and basic, is a tricky moral question.

By 1786 Burns was receiving critical acclaim for his poems, and he undertook a series of tours which continued into 1787. He met Clarinda, the sophisticated and well educated Mrs MacLehose, in Edinburgh late in 1787. The flirtation, by letter only (as Burns was confined to his lodgings with a leg injury), also inspired much lyricism. At this time Burns started his sustained contribution to James Johnson's *Scots Musical Museum* with many beautiful and still popular songs, reworked from the traditional body of Scottish folk song.

In 1788 he returned to Ayrshire and Jean Armour, who later produced twins again. He married her and moved to a farm, Ellisland, 10 km (6 miles) north of Dumfries. The next year he also took up employment with the Excise, though still struggling with the farm. This finally failed in 1791. He then worked full-time with the Excise, all the while contributing to further volumes of *Scots Musical Museum* and continuing his own poetic writings to support his growing family. As the 1790s progressed, he became intermittently ill and fell into low spirits. By 1795 he was ill with rheumatic fever, though struggling to keep up a supply of material for *A Select Collection of Original Scottish Airs for the Voice*. He died in July 1796 at Dumfries, where many relics of his life are to be seen today in Burns House, Burns Street, among other sites in the town.

Burns Suppers

On or around the poet's birth date of 25th January, Scots at home and abroad gather to celebrate their national poet. This celebration takes the form of a traditional meal of haggis with 'neeps' and 'tatties' (turnips and potatoes) and whisky. The haggis is solemnly brought to the top table accompanied by a piper. Burns' poem 'To a Haggis' is usually recited and at its conclusion the 'Great chieftain o' the Puddin-race' is ceremonially stabbed by the orator, with varying degrees of flair, perhaps depending on the amount of whisky consumed. (This is not quite as easy as it sounds. The haggis has a stretchy skin and, if not pierced properly, will tend to bounce off the plate and on to the floor.) The evening proceeds with toasts and speeches, the most important of which is to the Immortal Memory, celebrating the unique relationship which Scots have with their poet. There is usually also singing and reciting of Burns' works, either by specially invited guests or by the entire company.

One curious aspect of this phenomenon is how quickly after the poet's death the habit sprang up. The first official Burns Supper is thought to have been held at the Greenock Burns Club. The club itself started in 1801 and the following year the members held 'a comfortable dinner of which

Opposite: *Often described as Scotland's great champion, Sir Walter Scott's own vision of his native land came alive through his novels and poems. He popularised a romantic version of Scotland, peopled with noble clansmen. He was also responsible for the success of the visit of King George IV to Edinburgh in 1822 – an occasion which did much to popularise tartan as a fashionable cloth. This painting of him is by Sir William Allan.*

sheep's head and haggis formed an interesting part'. These days there is no longer a sheep's head, though the haggis is still a prerequisite. In 1805 another club was formed in Paisley, with the weaver poet Robert Tannahill as the secretary. By 1859 there were over 1,000 celebrations annually in various parts of the world. By 1885 these were being co-ordinated by the Burns Club Federation, whose headquarters are in Kilmarnock. (Not surprisingly, Burns Clubs near the poet's home ground are the most enthusiastically supported.) Today Burns Suppers are held not just by Burns Clubs as such, but by all kinds of organisations as part of their winter social calendar.

The essence of the Burns Supper is companionship and good humour (and whisky). Some are men-only affairs, though many are also decorous enough for both sexes. The appreciation of Burns is utterly unlike the academic adoration of, for example, Shakespeare; Burns speaks directly to Scots today, and he is loved more than ever for his foibles, his directness and his honest worth.

Robert Louis Stevenson

Robert Louis Stevenson (1850–94) differs from Sir Walter Scott and Robert Burns in that he travelled far beyond his native land, though he never forgot it. In spite of poor health, he achieved success in his own lifetime with classic adventure stories. Though abroad for much of his adult life, Stevenson's love for his country is warmly portrayed in all his writings.

The life of Stevenson

Born in Edinburgh in 1850 (8 Howard Place in the New Town) to a respectable, well-off family already noted for engineering work in connection with lighthouses and harbours, Stevenson did not follow the career expected of him and hence disappointed his parents. Instead he became unconventional, affecting a bohemian way of life at university. In 1875 he graduated in law, becoming an advocate, but never practised; he had resolved to be a writer instead.

Stevenson wrote his early works in the family's house at 17 Heriot Row, and at their cottage at Swanston. His father supported the struggling young author at this time but by 1877 he was working as a journalist in London and had become the centre of a literary and artistic circle. On one of his frequent tours of France, he met Mrs Fanny Osbourne, an independent and strong-minded American; he eventually followed her to California and married her in 1880. His health was meanwhile failing, damaged by the American voyage.

He returned to Europe in early 1881 with his wife and stepfamily and lived in a series of temporary homes, which included, in Scotland,

Opposite, left:
Though born into a famous engineering family, whose speciality was lighthouses, Robert Louis Stevenson's career was destined to be literary. Scotland's unpredictable climate did not suit Stevenson's delicate health and he travelled widely in Europe and the USA before eventually settling in Samoa. He never forgot his native land, which was a vivid setting for many of his most exciting novels. The painting of him here is by Count Girolamo Nerli.

Pitlochry in Perthshire, where his landlady had a store of ghostly High-land tales. One of them inspired the piece *Thrawn Janet*, written in broad Scots yet accepted by London's *Cornhill Magazine* and described by the American novelist Henry James as 'a masterpiece in thirteen pages'. Dur-ing the wet summer of 1881 the family moved from Pitlochry to Braemar, where perhaps Stevenson's most famous book, *Treasure Island*, flowed easily but hurriedly from his pen – the first 15 chapters in as many days.

Subsequently, for health reasons (his tubercular lung condition being made worse by the damp Scottish climate) he lived in Switzerland, the south of France and the south of England before eventually settling in Samoa in 1887. He remained there until his death in 1894, though he never forgot his native city. He died at only 44 – at an age when Sir Walter Scott was only just beginning to write the best of his romantic works.

Above right: Nobody else in Scottish literature inspires so much affection as Robert Burns, loved, in spite of the foibles of his personal life, and honoured annually in the popular tradition of Burns Suppers. His best works show him as an ironical observer of human nature and a poet in the down-to-earth folk tradition. This portrait of him was painted from life by Alexander Nasmyth in 1787.

Other famous Scots

If Burns, Scott and Stevenson are the best known of the Scots for their roles in literature, the worlds of commerce and science also produced some notable figures. From the time of the eighteenth-century Age of

This prospect of Edinburgh from Calton Hill is said to have been Robert Louis Stevenson's favourite view of his native city. Immediately right of the clock tower of the Balmoral Hotel is the Gothic spire of the Scott Monument, recalling another of Scotland's best-known literary figures.

Enlightenment – a movement in arts and science which was centred on Edinburgh in the decades following the loss of Scotland's independence – the nation gave to the world a number of statesmen, scientists and inventors out of all proportion to her size. Nobel prize-winning scientist Charles Wilson remarked of his fellow countrymen: 'the Scots in particular were possessed with that romantic speculative inventiveness, crossed with the mentality of a chartered accountant'. Hardheaded Scots making a name for themselves were such a commonly encountered type that they even came to be featured in great English literature. Donald Farfrae in Thomas Hardy's *The Mayor of Casterbridge* is just one example: a figure coolly in control of his destiny, contrasted with the central figure of Henchard, the mayor. The fictitious Farfrae, earning his living capably in the south of England, is a reminder of many real-life Scots, who for generations have had to emigrate to achieve anything at all.

90

The Scots abroad

Some left Scotland in extreme youth, their parents striking out for their New World. In this category falls John Muir (1838–1914) from Dunbar in East Lothian, a pioneering conservationist and founder of the American National Parks system. Even better known is Andrew Carnegie (1835–1918), who was the son of a poor weaver from Dunfermline near Edinburgh. From factory hand to railway clerk and telegraphist (where he became one of the first in the USA to be able to 'translate' the new-fangled signals down the wire into speech without having to write down the letters first), he later invested in oil, then in iron and steel. His investments grew to the extent that he eventually owned the largest iron and steel works in the world and lent his name to a special kind of philanthropy. His benefactions exceeded £70,000,000 and included libraries and various institutes throughout the USA and in Britain. He also made substantial gifts to, among other places, Dunfermline, including the town's park.

The lack of opportunity in Scotland, plus the enforced emigrations during the Clearances, encouraged the Scots to find new homes right across the globe. Sixty-three per cent of the commissioned officers of the Hudson Bay Company (the pioneering trading company in northern Canada) between 1821 and 1878 were Scots. Thirteen past Presidents of the USA had Scots blood, including Thomas Jefferson, James Monroe, Andrew Jackson, James Polk, James Buchanan, Andrew Johnson, Ulysses Grant, William McKinley, Theodore Roosevelt, Woodrow Wilson, Lyndon Johnson and Ronald Reagan. Nine of the signatories of the Declaration of Independence were Scots, including its author Charles Thomson, as well as James Wilson and the only cleric to sign, John Witherspoon. There are no less than 14 places around the globe called Aberdeen.

If poverty forced some Scots to emigrate, others held political views that made their homeland intolerable. Into this category comes Allan Pinkerton. Born in the urban slums of Glasgow, he eventually became a Chartist, fighting for social reform, but soon found it expedient to start afresh in the USA where he founded the world's largest investigation agency.

Another Scot who prospered abroad was William Jardine (1784–1843). He was a farmer's son from Lochmaben in Dumfriesshire who studied to become a surgeon and took a post with the East India Company on their far eastern trading ships. By 1817 he was an independent full-time China trader, subsequently setting up operations with another Scot, James Matheson, to form the company Jardine Matheson. The company became involved in what is seen today as a dreadful trade – the shipping of opium from India to China, by which means it amassed vast profits. The Chinese, their society greatly damaged over the passage of time by this appalling commerce, eventually took steps to stop the business. However, Jardine's political influence enabled him to persuade the British government of the day to retaliate when it seemed that this lucrative trade might be threatened. This episode became known as the First Opium War of

1841. When the Chinese sued for peace the British demanded the island of Hong Kong and, a few months later, Jardine Matheson and Company built the first permanent stone building of the new British colony. Perhaps William Jardine showed another Scottish characteristic – stubbornness – when he ever after refused to atone for his role in agitating for one of the least justifiable wars Britain ever engaged in.

Mathematicians and scientists

If Scots were helping to shape the world for good or ill, there were at least some who stayed at home but made their name in other ways. John Napier (1550–1617) was the eighth Laird of Merchiston and his name is still recalled in Napier College Edinburgh, literally built around the family's tower house. Napier was a phenomenal mathematician – he put the point into the decimal fraction and also invented logarithms, though some say that the massive task of computing exponential expressions was only undertaken because he was really looking for the number of the Beast of the Apocalypse – one of the obscure religious preoccupations of the time.

Later in Scotland's story, Scots made a substantial contribution to the world of science. James Clerk Maxwell (1831–79), son of a Dunfermline landowner, is now recognised as being second only to Einstein and Newton in his contribution to science. He worked on fundamental concepts to establish the properties of heat and gases. He founded the science of statistical mechanics and originated the notion of cybernetics (the comparative study of automatic communication and control, not just in living bodies but also in mechanical and electrical systems such as computers). He defined and introduced the idea of electro-magnetism, demonstrating the link between electricity and magnetism, and researched into the nature of light and colour, taking the world's first colour photograph while doing so.

Sir James Dewar (1847–1932), son of an inn-keeper in Kincardine, was an eminent scientist and inventor. One of his special areas of interest was in low temperature physics. To keep gases in a liquefied or low temperature state, he invented the vacuum flask in 1892. Eventually he met a German specialist glass blower called Reinhold Burger, whose knowledge enabled Dewar's design to be made stronger. Though Dewar was aware of the flask's property for keeping hot materials hot as well as his own requirement to keep cool things cool, he was not interested in the commercial possibilities; it was Burger who soon ensured that no picnic was complete without Dewar's invention.

William Thomson, Lord Kelvin (1824–1907) was an infant prodigy, a genius whose mathematics paper was read to the Royal Society of Edinburgh while he was still in his teens. (A suitably elderly professor was chosen to do the reading, as the learned society's members would not have been otherwise keen on such a youngster's work.) His wide-ranging later researches led him to be described as the father of nineteenth-century physics.

Scots names are found in units of measurements, such as in the degree kelvin, or the watt (while James Watt also found a way of measuring the power output of an engine and thus invented the notion of horsepower). Scots names are also recalled in scientific terms such as Graham's Law, about gas diffusion; Brewster's Law, concerning refractive indices (in optics); Brownian Movement, on the statistical fluctuations of the bombardment of molecules in solution; the Purdie Reaction, yet another term from chemistry; Maxwell's Demon, an imaginary creature with a pre-occupation for sorting out sizes of molecules in gases in order to break the second law of thermodynamics; also the Gordon-Rankine Formula, attributed singly or jointly to both men but chiefly concerned with calculating, in civil engineering, the collapsing load for a given column.

Medical men

Men of science overlap with men of medicine: the principle of dialysis on which kidney machines operate was evolved by a Glasgow chemist, Thomas Graham (1805–69). James Young Simpson (1811–70), who was bright enough to enter Edinburgh University at the tender age of 14, is remembered for his development of the anaesthetic. (If Simpson's methods had not been so successful then more might also have been heard of a certain James Easdale from Perth. In a hospital in India he performed the first successful operation using a technique of hypnosis.) Sir Alexander Fleming (1881–1955) is credited with the discovery of penicillin, while a whole generation of children have John Hughes Bennet (1812–75) to thank for his discovery of the beneficial effects of cod liver oil. From the use of lemon juice as a specific against scurvy (James Wood, 1716–94), to the description of the slipped disc (George Middleton, 1853–1923), Scots medical men have advanced knowledge on a broad front.

Engineers

In engineering, too, there were great advancements made by Scots. Poor Robert Mushet (1811–91) discovered the secret of cast steel, but neglected the patent rights. The name of Bessemer (an Englishman!) lives on in the Bessemer process of steelmaking – revolutionary in its day but prematurely announced. Bessemer's process was originally flawed because the steel produced had too high an oxygen content which made it fail under heat. Mushet built his own Bessemer-type furnace and added manganese ore to attract the oxygen away, thus producing the toughest steel yet known. Bessemer paid him a small annuity for his contribution but Mushet did not take out a patent – thus it was Bessemer who became the millionaire.

Thomas Telford (1757–1854) became one of the leading civil engineers of his age. In 18 years he oversaw the construction of 1,480 km (920 miles) of new road and 1,017 bridges in Scotland alone, as well as many projects south of the border. In one of his most ambitious projects, St Katherine's

James Watt and the Steam Engine was painted by R. S. Lauder around 1855. It was while working as a mathematical instrument maker at London University, that Greenock-born James Watt was given a working model of a Newcomen engine to repair. He quickly perceived this early pumping engine's defects and so improved it that he is often credited with the invention of the steam engine. He also patented numerous other mechanical and engineering devices.

Dock in London, England, he specified large steam pumps from his friend James Watt. This Greenock-born instrument maker improved the already existing Newcomen engine (which some argue was only a pump) and helped provide the means of powering the industrial revolution. It was his invention of the separate steam condenser which the Newcomen lacked, among other refinements, which resulted in the partly mistaken credit of the steam engine to Watt.

Other famous achievers

Scots were also responsible for the invention of a whole range of unlikely items, such as the first mechanical device to extrude spaghetti, the sack-sewing machine, the dog clutch, the centrifugal governor, the three-ply carpet loom and a host of other devices. From the bicycle (Kirkpatrick MacMillan, 1813–78) to the telephone (Alexander Graham Bell, 1847–1922) via the kitchen cupboard in which lurk Mrs Keillor's marmalade, James Johnston's Bovril, John Polson's cornflour and Lachlan Rose's lime-juice cordial, the fertile imaginations of the Scots have been at work. From the frankly bizarre (the first man to dissect an elephant was Patrick Blane, 1666–1728), to the everyday (the inventor of the eponymous macintosh, Charles Macintosh, 1786–1843, was a Glasgow chemical engineer), Scotland has produced a kaleidoscope of innovative talent put to practical use. And the kaleidoscope was invented by Sir David Brewster (1781–1868), an experimental scientist from Jedburgh in the Scottish Borders.

 SEVEN

SCOTTISH FOOD AND DRINK

What are the images that come to mind on the subject of Scottish food and drink? Haggis and oatmeal, venison and other game, salmon and sea trout, shortbread and home bakes, cakes and fancies, all washed down with whisky or Scottish liquors with recipes secret and mysterious – or even a nice cup of tea, as the Scots are reputed to be great tea drinkers. These are just a few of the products that are associated with Scotland both in the restaurant and at home on everyday occasions. But away from clever cuisine promoting A Taste of Scotland and in the face of supermarkets with their overwhelming buying power across Britain, as well as the spread of fast-food outlets and convenience foods, does a Scottish cuisine really survive as a recognisable home-grown feature? Is Scottish food different from that of the rest of the UK? Happily, the answer to both questions is yes.

The Auld Alliance in the kitchen

Scotland's historical links with France, and the tendency for Scots soldiers, men of letters and scientists to travel in Europe, ensured that Scotland's culinary traditions did not develop in isolation. Very early Scots cookery books described methods of dealing with fish and tongue after the Dutch and Polish styles respectively, but they emphasise French methods. King James I insisted on a French cook in his household. By the time of King James V and his French wife Mary of Lorraine, courtly cuisine was extremely sophisticated, and it continued so under Mary, Queen of Scots. Towards the end of the sixteenth century this 'high living' even resulted in food shortages in Scotland. Sir Richard Maitland (1496–1586) in his 'Satire on the Town Ladyes' comments that:

> . . . some will spend mair, I heir say,
> In spyce and droggis on ane day
> Than wad their mothers in ane yeir
> Whilk will gar mony pak decay   which will make fortunes decay
> When they sa vainlie waste thair geir.   goods

95

Perhaps here is heard the first notes of that Scottish puritanism which has, ever after, disapproved of the indulgences of the table. However, an interest in sophisticated cuisine was certainly maintained, partly through Jacobite links with France and the Continent, so that by the time of Robert Burns, who at birth was an ordinary Scot of Lowland farming stock, French culinary terms were quite familiar. Thus in his poem 'To a Haggis' he compares the humble, native Scots dish more than favourably to a French ragout or fricassee. Aside from the kitchens of the nobility and the well-to-do, and also the life of the tavern in cities, the typical cottage kitchen of Burns' time would have included many items with French links. Milk and provisions were kept in the 'aumry' or cupboard (from the French *armoire*). On the dresser or kitchen sideboard (from French *dressoir*) could be seen the cutlery and crockery, including the 'ashet' or serving plate (from French *assiette*), a selection of 'tassies' or cups (French *tasse*) and possibly a 'verry' or glass (French *verre*). Many of these terms survive in Scotland today, though some have all but disappeared.

The kitchen's focus was the open hearth, where the cooking utensils were hung, perhaps most importantly the girdle (griddle) for the oatcakes and the 'sooty bannocks' (sauté bannocks – French again!). Also in use would be the kale-pot, the all-purpose pot on three legs that could also serve as an oven when buried in hot peats. Typically, the kitchen also contained the plunge churn (used for making cheese), the spinning wheel, the muckle chair (best chair) and creepie stools (three-legged stools for creeping up to the fire).

Food contrasts in time and place

Historically, what Scotland ate depended on locality, season and social class. For the well-to-do in sixteenth-century Scotland, the nation's well established trading links across the North Sea ensured that the resources of home could be supplemented by dainties and spices brought in from abroad. No laird or Highland chief went without his fine claret from France or his hogshead of imported sherry to supplement the local distillations.

Documentary evidence of the less well off in seventeenth-century Scotland includes a complete inventory of foodstuffs in the kitchen found in the poem 'The Blythesome Bridal', thought to be by Sir Robert Sempill of Beltrees, Renfrewshire (*c*.1595–*c*.1660). Admittedly this includes the food for a wedding celebration, but it is notable for its emphasis on fish and also oats, as opposed to red meat. Amongst its bannocks and its salt herring and its barrels of ale, its spring onions, radishes and peas can also be found:

> . . . tartan, dragen and brochan
> And fouth o guid gabbocks o skate,

Powsoudie, and drammock, and crowdie,
And caller nowt-feet on a plate.
And there'll be partans and buckies,
And speldins and haddocks enew,
And singit sheep heads and a haggis,
And scadlips to sup till ye're fou.

This is but one of four verses and even some native Scots will have difficulty in noting that this verse alone mentions five different preparations of oatmeal, plus skate and smoked haddock in variety, as well as crabs and winkles and a sheep's head, not only singed, but served as soup as well (that is the 'powsoudie' part). The 'scadlips', a barley broth, is intended to fill up the corners, or alternatively the guests can nibble on fresh ox-feet. It is notable that with the haggis, and the head and feet, the meat cuts are certainly inexpensive.

If this is a diet worth celebrating, then at the other extreme, the Royal Commission under Lord Napier, set up in 1883 to investigate the life of the crofters in the Highlands and islands, found many instances of hardship and monotony. They learned, for example, that on the Shetland island of Foula even potatoes grew poorly and that all crops were frequently ruined by salt-laden gales so that only 'bere' (primitive barley) could survive. One Islander commented 'there is nothing here but the point of the hook to turn to', meaning that only the hazardous sea fishery sustained them.

Oatmeal as a staple

Though that was an extreme example in every sense, the diet of the Scots was certainly bound up with locality. In one respect, those islanders were fortunate, as fish was seldom tasted by the farm workers far up-country in the heyday of the 'ferm-touns' – the improved farms of the Lowland and Lowland edge. Their staple was oatmeal, just as it had been that of the Highlander on many an upland trek with cattle in the old days of cattle droving. In fact, until well into the present century in agricultural Lowland Scotland, oatmeal was almost a kind of currency. The rural minister expected it as part of his stipend, as did the 'dominie' (schoolmaster). And if the Scottish education system produced the 'lad o pairts', meaning a bright but underprivileged pupil who could proceed to further education, then the Scottish universities had a holiday known as Meal Monday, intended for the rural student to make his way home to pick up his supplies of oatmeal for the remainder of the term. At least, that is the story. It certainly illustrates the important part oatmeal played in the Scots diet.

In its simplest form oatmeal was made into brose. This is simply oatmeal mixed with hot water, with salt and pepper for flavour and added milk or

97

cream if available. In the 'bothies' (unmarried farmhands' quarters) of some Scottish farms it constituted breakfast, dinner and supper. By way of variation, kale or turnip might be added, but meat was seldom eaten except on special days – some of these are described in the next chapter. Hence the preoccupation with food which turns up in the bothy ballads – the pithy work songs composed by the farmhands:

The breid was thick, the brose was thin	bread
and the broth it was like bree	brine
I chased the barley roon the plate	
and aa I got was three.	all

Kale

From the eighteenth-century improvements until well into the present century, the married farmhand or cottar was a little better off than the bothy lad. He had a small plot of land on which a few vegetables and potatoes could be grown. The commonest vegetable was kale, which could survive the Scottish winter. In fact kale's former importance in the Scottish diet can be judged from the variety of phrases which mention it. The kaleyard school is the name applied to an uncomfortably sentimental set of Scottish writers in the late nineteenth century whose subjects were cosy and parochial. 'Cauld kale het up' (cold kale heated up) is an old tale revived, while kale itself is still used in the sense of food in general or in some places soup (which would have been mostly kale anyway!). Curiously, kale was very much a Lowland dish. The Highlander used nettle instead in his broth, regarding the eating of kale as a positively effeminate characteristic. The Grants, for example, living on Speyside near the Lowland edge, were referred to by their opponents as the soft, kale-eating Grants and a Gaelic poem celebrating the Jacobite/Highland victory at Killiecrankie refers to the defeated forces as 'men of kale and brose'.

Oats and more oats

As working conditions improved in the countryside, the cottars' employment terms with the farmer would often have included not only oatmeal but also milk and tatties (potatoes). In those days, in the single man's bothy, married couple's cottar house, or in the manse or schoolhouse, farm kitchen and probably mansion as well, one of the most important household items would have been the girnal, a chest for keeping the oatmeal. In many households, filling the girnal had an almost ritualistic quality. It had to be tramped or pressed down in order both to fit into the chest and to ensure it kept its flavour and moistness. If the French had their grape pressing, then the Scots likewise had their oatmeal trampling. When the meal sack was delivered from the local mill, the children of the house, the farm's 'orra loon' (spare hand), or even the kitchen lass herself, after washing of feet, packed down the meal into its chest.

However, times have moved on. No longer is oatmeal the staple it once

Opposite: *The interior of this black house on Lewis contains some of the traditional implements and crockery found in a Highland kitchen of former times. It has been preserved by Historic Scotland.*

was, and meal chests and barrels turn up in antique shops instead. Yet the humble oat still has its role in contemporary Scots cuisine. Porridge can be seen as the slightly more deluxe version of brose which turns up on the menu of even the smallest Scottish bed-and-breakfast. Oats also can be found in skirlie, a basic dish of oatmeal fried in some form of animal fat or suet with onions. Oats even make a healthy coating for fish (herrings and oatmeal turn up as a bar lunch) and find their way into ice cream and local fruit-based sweet courses, where the flaky, nutty texture adds extra bite.

Haggis

Oatmeal naturally finds its way into haggis, probably the best known Scottish dish. It consists of a sheep or lamb's stomach bag, stuffed with oatmeal, suet, liver, stock, minced hearts and lights of a sheep, onion, pepper and salt. The ingredients probably explain why few, if any, Scots make it at home now, though it is widely available from Scottish butchers (though sometimes the outer skin is plastic). A few enterprising butchers also make vegetarian haggis. Cheap and nourishing, haggis manages to be an everyday dish yet at the same time fulfils its ritual part in Burns Supper celebrations. Scotland's enterprising hoteliers sometimes serve a mini portion of it as a starter, for the edification of non-Scots who want to return home with the boast of having tried it.

Beef

Perhaps the name most associated with Scottish beef is Aberdeen Angus – the byword for quality. Its story goes all the way back to the time of a certain Hugh Watson, born in 1789, a farmer with expertise in picking out the best characteristics of the small black cattle (the usual Highland sort at that time). During the first half of the nineteenth century, he set out to build a champion herd at his farm at Keillor in Angus. He knew the publicity value of the show ring and soon his cattle were developing an impressive reputation. Even Prince Albert bought them, with Queen Victoria's full approval!

The Aberdeenshire connection comes from a farmer called William McCombie who was pursuing similar aims of breeding the very highest quality beasts from native stock. Though Watson in Angus did vital pioneering work in bringing together the best strains, it was McCombie who was to strengthen the strain and actually improve on Watson's record in the showground.

This tradition of the highest quality was continued by Sir George Macpherson Grant of Ballindalloch on Speyside into the early years of the present century. By the late nineteenth century the Aberdeen Angus

breed was world famous, and it was eventually exported to more than 60 countries worldwide. Today its particular attributes of high quality lean meat, from an outstandingly hardy and easily fed animal, are still sought after.

Venison

As for venison, it is an important high quality product of the vast sporting estates of the north. It still carries, to a certain extent, an exclusive tag, and in particular is popular with restaurant and hotel chefs in Scotland. Most of it comes from red deer, whose natural habitat is the forest, although it has now adapted in Scotland to life mostly on the open hill where, in the absence of natural enemies such as the wolf, it is kept at unnaturally high numbers. This benefits the estates and their sporting clients, though hardly the regeneration of Scotland's natural woodlands. Some venison also comes from the smaller roe deer, which are very common in forestry plantations in many parts of Scotland. The best meat for roasting, chefs maintain, comes from a young stag which has been taken well into the autumn.

Game on the wing

Scottish game birds include the well known red grouse, a denizen of moorlands. These are usually 'managed', which involves burning the heather moor in strips in rotation to ensure plentiful supplies of young heather shoots, the bird's main food. One grouse gives a portion for one person and thus it is a quarry with more prestige than meat. On this aristocratic bird hinges the yearly ritual of the 'Glorious Twelfth', that is, the 12th August or start of the grouse-shooting season, and the annual preoccupation with the task of ensuring that these Highland morsels find their way promptly to the dining tables of the best hotels and restaurants. Other examples of the game bird family which very occasionally may be found on the menu include the ptarmigan, a high-altitude grouse whose white-winged summer coloration and ridiculous tameness render it somewhat unsporting, and the capercailzie, a large and very noisy game bird whose current rare status is causing conservationists concern. In Lowland Scotland, pheasant and partridge are widespread and often find their way into the chef's kitchen, as does pigeon.

Angler's delight

Yet another component in Scotland's sporting economy is salmon. This was at one time a common food, but both damming and pollution have affected the species in many parts of its range. The low levels of pollution in Scotland, especially in the Highlands and other non-industrial areas, mean that it has fared better here, particularly as fish ladders and bypasses have been incorporated into many hydroelectric schemes. (The most famous of these is probably at Pitlochry, just a few minutes from the main street, where the fish leap by stages up their ladder then swim through a pipe with a glass observation panel cut into it.)

Controversy over conservation measures working to the advantage of salmon-angling syndicates flares up in Scotland from time to time. In fact, any conservation legislation is made complex by the extraordinary life cycle of the salmon. They are born into the gravelly clarity of a Highland burn then take to the sea, usually in their second year. From there they return to their own home burn to spawn, anything from one to four years later. It is those salmon, sleek and well-muscled from their sojourn in the rich Atlantic, that are avidly sought after by those who can afford them. The desirable pinkness of the flesh of the salmon comes from absorbing the pigment from certain crustaceans, which it finds at sea. This marine habit is shared by its close cousin the sea trout, which is really only a brown trout that has developed a desire to go beyond its Scottish burn or loch and hence has run away to sea. In general, it is less expensive to fish these river trout than salmon, but they share the same characteristic of making succulent eating.

Sea harvest

Scotland's sea fishery has in recent years brought great wealth to a number of east coast Lowland ports; Peterhead is now the largest white-fish landing port in Europe. In Scotland today there exists the curious anomaly that the very best of fish, particularly shellfish, is often exported to Europe, especially France. However, there are certainly some outstanding fish restaurants in Scotland where dedicated chefs cultivate – almost secretly – their local suppliers.

By the nineteenth century the fishery had begun to develop in volume, and though railways certainly helped open up the market there was still a wide range of ways of preserving fish for both local consumption and export. Some are still found today. Dr Johnson tried, if not enjoyed, speldings – north-east sun-and-wind-dried small haddock or whiting. These were particularly associated with the village of Collieston, north of Aberdeen.

Elsewhere, cod, split and opened up, were sometimes literally hung on the washing line to be air dried, though the habit is much less widespread

Opposite: Game such as pheasant and salmon often feature prominently in sophisticated dining in Scotland. Likewise other local vegetables and soft fruits bring a freshness to the dinner menu. Your host may offer a dram afterwards – a high quality single malt whisky (surpassing any French brandy) and, as petits fours, dainty chocolate-coated triangles of Walkers Shortbread.

today. The smoking of fish certainly continues in Scotland, not just to make kippers from herring, but also the well known Arbroath smokie (a split smoked haddock), or the finnan haddie (a similar treatment associated with Findon, a former fishing village just south of Aberdeen). Smoked fish is often eaten in Scotland for breakfast as visitors at a Scottish bed-and-breakfast establishment will find. Another Scottish speciality, still common in the fishing community and frequent on the menus of good fish restaurants, is skate.

In earlier days, Scotland also had an important herring fishery. A salted keg of west coast herring was a popular gift (these plump western herring were often jocularly referred to as 'Glasgow magistrates'). The east coast herring fishery also became very important, with a herring season starting in early spring in Shetland and moving down the coast as the year went on; the girls who gutted, salted and packed the herring went with the fleet.

Much promoted by hoteliers keen to offer an authentic taste of Scotland is a dish called Cullen Skink. This recalls the attractive little Banffshire community of Cullen and is a traditional local recipe for a thick and creamy smoked fish soup. The name may or may not be an ironic reference to the poor fare of former days – as skink can mean in Scots a thin wishy-washy liquid (from Middle-English *skynke* meaning to pour, usually wine). However, perhaps more common is the meaning of a shin of beef (from the Dutch *schenke*, a shin or ham – c.f. shank). It seems to suggest that the poor fisher folk of Cullen could not even afford the cheapest cut of meat and had to make do with fish. If so, then it parallels another Scots term for herring: twa-eyed steak!

Soft climate, soft fruits

With perhaps a fish starter and a game main course, a formal Scottish dinner at a good restaurant can move on to locally produced sweets. The climate around Dundee, north of the Tay, over the Sidlaw Hills, down into Strathmore and taking in Blairgowrie, offers just the right mix of sunshine, mildness and soft summer rain to produce the finest of soft fruits. In fact, the area around Strathmore is the main soft-fruit-growing area in the EEC. Raspberries are the chief of the soft fruit clan and they bring the sharp-sweet taste of a northern summer to a variety of desserts. Typical of these is Tipsy Laird, a simple dish of fresh raspberries soaked in whisky and served on a sponge base with whipped cream.

The proximity of Dundee to all this fruit growing was a major factor in the growth of a jam-making industry within the city. Dundee is also associated with marmalade, using oranges not from Strathmore but from Seville. It is said that in 1700 a small grocer called James Keillor bought a cargo of bitter Seville oranges going cheap at the port and his wife used a recipe originally intended for a quince preserve. This eventually led to the opening of the world's first marmalade production plant in 1797 by one of his descendants.

Scottish cheeses

If the Scottish diner prefers to stay with something savoury to finish a meal, there are plenty of Scottish cheeses worth sampling. Oatmeal makes another appearance as a coating for the very rich Caboc, made with double cream. This brand borrows the formerly general word for cheese, kebbock (variously spelt), which sometimes still occurs in Scots as a kebbock of cheese, meaning a whole cheese, or the kebbock-heel, meaning the rind or end-piece.

In former days, making 'farmhouse cheese' was an activity carried out in many rural locations. Today, other priorities claiming the farm-wife's time and official regulations have reduced the number of cheeses made in Scotland. Along with the ubiquitous Scottish cheddar (a geographical contradiction) made by various Scottish creameries, Dunlop is one of the better known names in Scottish cheese-making today. Orkney is also notable for its mainly creamery-made cheeses, though some are still made on local farms. Crowdie, a fresh skimmed cow's milk cheese, is produced on the mainland with a variety of flavourings. More specialist cheeses include the sought-after Lanark Blue, made with ewe's milk, which turns up in speciality cheese shops and a few good restaurants, and Dunsyre Blue, a cow's milk cheese. Bonchester Bridge is a Brie-type cheese from the Scottish Borders. Other regional variations, both on cheddar-style hard cheese and crowdie-type soft cheeses, are also to be found.

A tradition of baking

With the mention of sweet things, Scottish cuisine, from humble home bake to smart restaurant kitchen, unites as if in a common purpose. It is worth noting that the notion of dessert – from the French *desservir*, meaning to clear or to take away (i.e. the main course) – came into use in Scotland in the sixteenth century. In England, it was not until the middle of the following century that the idea took root. This gave the Scots at least 100 years' start in developing their unashamed sweet tooth and practising the art of sweet-making and baking.

Scones (in Scotland pronounced to rhyme with lawns) are just one component of the Scottish institution of high tea. This is a substantial afternoon tea, bulked by a main course of perhaps fish or grilled steak and

sometimes soup, followed by an array of cakes and fancies, all taken with tea – a beverage introduced to Scotland by Mary of Modena, wife of King James VII and II. In the best circles the tea-making ritual developed into afternoon tea because the men, in particular, felt the need for some sustenance to go with this new-fangled fashionable drink. This in turn became high tea, with the addition of a hot dish. It is generally served before, say, 6 o'clock and seems designed to allow the Scots baker a stage to display his or her baking skills.

The high esteem for those who bake at home certainly also extends to the good baker's shop. As time went by, fewer and fewer households baked their own bread, for economic and historical reasons which were certainly connected with the drift away from being a rural society. The town or village baker therefore had an increasingly important function. However, professional bakers in Scotland would have been originally influenced by French methods – another aspect of the Auld Alliance. In any event, being patronised at first only by the wealthier townsfolk and nobility, they would have used only the finest of ingredients. This early-established tradition of excellence in the best bakers was handed down through the generations.

Thus, when Joseph Walker opened his baker's shop in 1898, he was able both to draw on a wealth of bakery experience and to lay down high standards of quality. Not only did he succeed in doing this, but more than 80 years later the tradition of excellence is maintained by the third generation of Walkers, Joseph, James and Marjorie, Joseph's grandchildren. The concern for the pure ingredients used by the small traditional baker remains the same – only the scale of the operation in Aberlour has been enlarged.

Walkers Shortbread: inheriting the tradition

In many of the products baked today by Walkers, strands of Scottish history and tradition run together. Shortbread is Scottish, pure and simple, reflecting not just the Scots' happy association with tasty sweet things, but in at least one of its varieties, Petticoat Tails, echoing the old French connections. The name is likely to be from *petites gatelles* – at least this is the straightforward explanation – but look a little further and all sorts of Scottish byways can be followed. An early mention (1826) of the derivation is in *The Cook and Housewife's Manual* written by Meg Dods. However, this was really the pen-name of a certain Mrs Isobel Johnston, wife of an Edinburgh publisher. The introduction to her work was probably written by Sir Walter Scott, who in his writing invented a mythical dining club, the Cleikum Club, presided over by the equally fictional Meg. She, in turn, was modelled on a real-life Miss Marian Ritchie, who was the tyrannical landlady of the Cross Keys Inn in Peebles. Meanwhile, Meg's fictional life was perpetuated by her reappearance in Scott's novel *St Ronan's Well*! Not only does the above demonstrate Scott's fine facility for blending fact, fiction and tradition together, it also demonstrates the

Opposite: *The fashion of tea drinking soon led to the introduction of afternoon tea, meaning the addition of some substantial fare to the tea-making ritual. In Scotland, this gave bakers a fine opportunity to develop their skills, which probably explains why Walkers' products appear on many a tea-table throughout the land.*

107

difficulty of drawing hard conclusions. As if to tease, the Annals of the Cleikum Club also point out that the circular shape of Petticoat Tails, baked in the round, is also the shape of the bell-hoop petticoats of former times! In Scotland it seems that not even the shortbread is without controversy.

In any event, shortbread recipes in old Scots' cookbooks take in many different kinds and, sure enough, Walkers' own baking displays not only Petticoat Tails, but also traditional rounds, triangles and fingers, as well as fine shortbread with the addition of chocolate chip or dark chocolate coating, almonds, hazelnuts or stem ginger – simple, pure natural flavours added to the basic wholesome ingredients. Tradition comes up to date with Walkers' own wholemeal shortbread, reflecting the 1990s trend for high-fibre eating.

Given the Scots' long association with oatmeal, already described in this chapter, Walkers also make a range of oatcakes. Although far from being the staple of former days, they are enjoying a revival due to an increasing interest in health. They now accompany a range of savoury foods, especially cheeses and pâtés, as well as honey and jams. However, the special qualities of oatcakes have been celebrated since earliest times:

The carline brought her kebbuck ben	old woman/cheese
Wi girdle-cakes weel toasted broon	oatcakes/brown
Weel does the canny kimmer ken	gossip know
They gar the scuds gae glither doon	ale go down easier

Traditional song: 'Andro and his Cutty Gun'

Today's oatcake consumers, canny kimmers or not, can enjoy Walkers' oatcakes made with traditional pinhead oatmeal, or a lighter oatcake as well as sophisticated cocktail oatcakes, the modern-trend bran oatcakes, and also Crofters oatcakes, their characteristic triangular shape a reminder of the days when girdle-fired round cake or bannock was cut into quarters. This brings us to the Scots word for these oatcakes: 'farles' or 'fardels', from Old English *feorth-dail* or fourth part.

When Robert Burns described Scotland as 'The Land o Cakes', he originally meant oatcakes, but as a wider definition it certainly holds true today. The traditional Scottish tea was and still is the proving ground for quality bakers (perhaps literally in the Scots' use of the word 'pruive' or 'preein', meaning to sample by taste). Not content with its association with marmalade, Dundee by the late nineteenth century had also given its name to a kind of rich cake, characterised not only by its generous quantities of dried fruits, peel and spices but also by the liberal scattering of blanched almonds on top. Walkers' own recipe retains all the special attributes of lightness, full flavour and good keeping qualities appreciated by generations of Scots hostesses. Likewise the rest of the Walkers' range of baked cakes follow the first principles of using only the best of ingredients without any artificial flavourings, just as the Scottish cook at home would. Highland and Strathspey Fruit Cake, Paradise Cake and Scotch

Bun – each echoing with their special ingredients of finest flour and butter, full-flavoured spices and fruit, the tradition of baking for special occasions – are festive cakes for celebrations of all kinds. In fact Black Bun is still traditionally associated with the Scots Hogmanay. Cakes rich or savoury, fruity or oaty, played their part in Scotland's ancient patterns of festivals and fairs.

The Scots at breakfast

Finally, lest the impression be given that the highlight of Scots cuisine is high tea, others might argue that the Scots peak early in the day thanks to the traditional Scots breakfast, that robust send-off of traditional guest houses and bed-and-breakfast establishments the length of the country. 'In the breakfast', pontificates Dr Johnson during his visit to Scotland, 'the Scots . . . must be confessed to excel us. The tea and coffee are accompanied not only with butter, but with honey, conserves and marmalades. If an epicure could remove by a wish in quest of sensual gratification . . . he would breakfast in Scotland.' Presumably, Johnson was only describing the extras – though even today's 'traditional breakfast' has contracted a little from descriptions of spreads laid out for guests in the well-to-do mansions of eighteenth-century Scotland, where plates of smoked beef, salt herrings, smoked salmon and other palatable delights took their place. However, the average bed-and-breakfast or hotel will provide a substantial breakfast consisting of, for example, omelette, smoked fish, bacon, eggs, black pudding, mushrooms and fried bread.

It seems that before the days of tea and coffee, even stronger beverages were offered. Writing in 1729, the Highlander Mackintosh of Borlum laments, 'When I come to a friend's house of a morning, I used to be asked if I had had my morning draught yet. I am now asked if I have had my tea.' Mackintosh complains that instead of 'the big quaich [Gael *cuach*, cup or bowl] with strong ale' all he gets is a cup of tea with fripperies like silverware and china as well as 'marmalade and cream'.

Mackintosh is clearly being unfair. He was probably plied with food as a token of the household's affection for him. In fact, the serving of even so much as a cup of tea without anything to eat is almost unthinkable in many Scots' homes even to this day, especially in rural areas. The concept of serving tea and coffee with absolutely nothing else is possibly a surviving English practice, now to be noted north of the border. For many Scots of an older generation, not given to outward expression of affection, offering food in plenty is almost a show of deep feelings.

Traditional drinks

Thanks to the weight of modern-day marketing campaigns there is an inescapable association of Scotland and whisky, almost to the exclusion of other beverages. Yet in former times, Scots certainly imbibed a wide range of drinks, potent or otherwise. Links with France ensured that wines were at one time among Scotland's principal imports. If contemporary accounts are to be believed, these reached their peak of consumption in eighteenth-century Edinburgh, especially in the inns and taverns of the Royal Mile, where the degree of insobriety was spectacular.

Writing around 1823, Robert Chambers (a name still recalled in today's *Chambers Dictionaries*) remarks that, 'Tavern dissipation, now so rare among the respectable classes of the community, formerly prevailed in Edinburgh to an incredible extent, and engrossed the leisure hours of all professional men, scarcely excepting even the most stern and dignified'. He goes on to relate in his *Traditions of Edinburgh* a variety of tales of learned men and their capacity to mop up strong drink: the greatly esteemed judge best fitted for his job only after downing six bottles of claret; another dignified and senior member of the legal profession who, after an outstanding evening's imbibing, was found asleep in a shed used by the local sweep; a game of cards between four lawyers which only ended with the three visitors being ushered into the street by the fourth who by this time had struggled into his nightshirt and nightcap and held a candle aloft to guide their path from his door. This fact was widely remarked by the forenoon churchgoers on their way past in broad daylight. Good French claret was usually the culprit, with 'small claret' sold incredibly cheaply at twenty pence for a Scottish pint, or ten pence a bottle!

Robert Burns enjoyed tavern life as much as anyone. Yet his song of praise 'Scotch Drink' is more a celebration of ale – 'I sing the juice Scotch bear can mak us' – and a reminder that beer and ale are still associated with Scotland, which has its own vocabulary for describing or ordering beers in the pubs of today. The use of the word bitter when ordering a dark beer in Scotland will instantly mark the user as an incomer or southerner! As for other ales, it is said that the ancient Picts were fired up on a particularly potent form of heather ale. The recipe of this fighting brew died with them when they were finally conquered by the Scots, according to the Scottish historian Hector Boethius (1465–1536), but persistent rumours that it is still being made survive, including one from Islay in the eighteenth century which is noted by the traveller Thomas Pennant. A near-contemporary recipe for it includes hops, golden syrup, yeast and ginger – perhaps not all to be found in a Pictish store-cupboard – as well as a large pot full of freshly cut tops of heather in full bloom.

Traditionally, other raw materials were made into wine or ale in Scotland. Glasgow Punch, a popular drink in the eighteenth and nineteenth

Opposite: The phrase 'traditional Scottish breakfast' is seen on many hotel and guest-house menus and is the rule rather than the exception in most bed-and-breakfast establishments. It means a hearty cooked meal intended to fortify the visitor for the rigours of sightseeing or for more strenuous pursuits such as hillwalking.

111

centuries when Glasgow was a successful mercantile centre, was rum-based. It used limes and lemons, presumably as these were items which the 'tobacco barons' and other successful merchants trading with the West Indies from Glasgow could easily lay their hands on. The juice or sap of the birch tree was another source of a wine, again according to Pennant, with a recipe later refined by the addition of raisins and almonds. Similarly, hops and molasses formerly made a treacle ale, while oatmeal almost inevitably found its way into a range of drinks, alcoholic or otherwise.

'Wi usquabae, we'll face the devil!'

So wrote Burns in 'Tam o' Shanter', referring to the Gaelic *uisge beatha*, translated as water of life, which becomes whisky in Scots. Amongst his many references to the drink, he even acknowledges it (in 'Scotch Drink' again) as an inspiration for better rhyming:

> O Whisky! soul o plays an pranks!
> Accept a Bardie's grateful thanks!
> When wanting thee, what tuneless cranks
> Are my poor Verses!

For centuries the Highlanders produced *uisge beatha* long before it became an internationally renowned drink, reserving it at first for special occasions. Some say it was the punitive taxes on imported wines that encouraged its manufacture. Nowadays, whisky is one of the most important and characteristic Scottish exports. Yet there is still an element of mystery about the making of malt whisky from the simple ingredients of barley, water and peat.

There are two main types of whisky, malt and grain. Malt whisky has a more pronounced flavour and bouquet, and hence an exclusive tag. It is made with malted barley. Grain whisky also contains malted barley, with unmalted barley and maize. Blended whisky is exactly as its name suggests, a combination of malt and grain whiskies, with de luxe blends containing more malts. Malts are sometimes classified into four main types: Highland, Lowland, Islay (from the island) and Campbeltown (meaning from the Mull of Kintyre). The Campbeltown malts are no longer significant and thus it is simpler to categorise only two general types: the malt whisky made in the east of Scotland, such as Speyside, which tends to be lighter or sweeter, and the island or western malts, which often have an easily recognisable taste of peat-smoke.

Scotland's whisky manufacturers have long realised the advantage in placing their name before the market by opening up their distilleries for visitors. Around 30 major distilleries with visitor centres offering a tour and a tasting (at least) are available in Scotland today – a small fraction of the total number of distilleries.

The overwhelming impression on visiting a distillery may be of the fascinating smell that the process has at each stage. Fall into conversation with a professional whisky blender and he will probably tell you that his

own nose is highly insured. He may also tell you that the correct way to drink whisky is with just a little water. If a visitor to Scotland, then you are obviously entitled to drink it any way you like, but beware of asking for lemonade or ginger if your host or hostess decides you are worthy of a dram of their best malt – native Scots can be a little touchy if their finest and favourite tipple is tainted before their eyes.

Nevertheless there is a long and honourable tradition in adding other ingredients to whisky. Most folk have heard of a toddy, which may recall Tod's Well near Arthur's Seat in Edinburgh, which was once a main source of Edinburgh's water supply. (Presumably the fact that the name attached itself to the whisky-based drink suggests the extent to which the two ingredients, water and whisky, were found together in Edinburgh.) Toddy means the addition of sugar or even lemon juice and honey to the dram. Athole Brose, traditionally drunk at Hogmanay by the officers and sergeants of the Argyll and Sutherland Highlanders, has honey and pure water added to its whisky base and must be stirred with a silver spoon. Auld Man's Milk, a Meg Dods recipe, is a concoction which uses eggs and cream, nutmeg and lemon in a cocktail of rum, brandy and whisky. This rocket fuel mix is innocently described in an old recipe book as a morning dram (unless it is a misprint for a morning drama!). In Caledonian Liquor, Highland Cordial, Scots Noyau and many more, the Scots of old cheerfully mixed whisky to their own taste. Meg Dods describes the ritual of making Het Pint, carefully adding three eggs to warm ale with sugar and nutmeg, then lacing it with whisky to make a special drink not only for Hogmanay, but for other special occasions such as marriages, where it would be drunk from a large wooden vessel called the bride's 'coggie'. At this point food and drink merge with festival and tradition as an integral part of both – and more can be found on this in the next chapter.

Part Three
Scottish Festivals and Folklore

 EIGHT

A YEAR OF TRADITIONS AND CUSTOMS

At first sight the everyday life of Scotland seems to have swept aside the customs of the past. But look closer and these old traditions can still be seen, sometimes as minor events, at other times in various parts of the nation as a major diversion for a day or so. Climbing to the high tops of mountains at midsummer, burning Viking longships, guisers round the door, fire festivals and the special baking of rich cakes all play their part in a way of life which echoes and acknowledges the old ways.

Yuletide and Hogmanay

> Rise up, auld wifie, and shak your feathers,
> Dinna think that we are beggars;
> For we are bairns come out to play,
> Rise up and gie us our Hogmanay.

The best-known festival, and one that is celebrated nation-wide, is Hogmanay, the 31st December. The name is thought to relate to the north French dialect word *hoginane*, meaning 'a gift at the New Year'. However, it has also been suggested that it is French dialect *au gui menez*, meaning 'to the mistletoe go', formerly cried by mummers; or, equally plausibly, *au geux menez*, meaning 'bring to the beggars', a reminder of the giving of gifts associated with this time of year.

Until very recently Hogmanay was probably the most important celebration in the Scottish calendar, and for some Scots it still is. At one time it all but eclipsed Christmas for many in Scotland. Now, because of the mostly English-based broadcasting media as well as high street stores UK-wide, Christmas is probably celebrated as much north of the border as in the south, though the Scots tend to hold a bit of their festive spirit back for Hogmanay.

It is thought that the Scots' preoccupation with Hogmanay came about

116

because of the efforts of the Presbyterian church, after the Reformation, to extinguish all Catholic holy days of which the Feast of the Nativity – that is, Christmas – was the principal. The Hogmanay celebration of the passing beyond midwinter to a time of lengthening daylight is surely grafted on to very early traditions. The ancient Druid priests are said to have initiated the festival of Yuletide, which in Scotland became 'the hallowed days of Yule' of the balladeers, covering Hogmanay and the first week of January. The Norse also had their own midwinter season of Jul, which actually continued for 24 days and included the winter solstice. In rural areas especially, up to the 1950s, possibly even more recently, many factories and other work places stayed open on Christmas Day, although all closed for the New Year. Children, particularly in the east coast fishing communities, hung up their stockings at Hogmanay, secure in the knowledge that Santa Claus (never Father Christmas) would work a late shift especially for their benefit.

Pages 114–15: Many sightings of the Loch Ness monster have been made from the vicinity of Urquhart Castle. Once one of the largest in Scotland, this strategic fortress in the Great Glen was blown up in 1692 to prevent it falling into Jacobite hands.

Hogmanay rituals

Habits change with each succeeding generation. The stroke of midnight on the 31st December once carried with it a great weight of ritual which varied from place to place, and survives to varying degrees. The household fire, the very symbol of life and warmth in the long bleak nights of a northern winter, had to be tended so that it was blazing brightly at midnight. This ensured sufficient prosperity in the household to keep the fire lit for the next 12 months. In some places the door of the household was opened to let out the old year, then closed as the chimes of midnight died away. In others, it was flung open to welcome in the New Year. Ships in dock still sound their sirens as in former times, while in the days of steam locomotives, any in steam at the depot at midnight were likewise given a blast of the whistle.

Other time-honoured practices included acknowledging New Year by wearing something new and cleaning the house thoroughly to make it look like new and so ready for the New Year. The custom of 'first footing' still survives. Ideally, the first visitor over the threshold after midnight should be a dark and handsome male stranger bearing gifts, particularly those connected with food or the hearth. The dark complexion of the first foot is considered important. Redheads are not considered a good omen, and women are also thought unlucky. Sometimes the household resorts to pushing out into the cold night any half-presentable male who happens to be in the house just before midnight, re-admitting him with his symbols of light and warmth. Peat (particularly in the Highlands) and coal were commonly used as symbols of household comfort and warmth; and some Scots keep the tradition alive today by solemnly entering a household with a small, perhaps carefully washed, piece of smokeless fuel.

As for other symbolic gifts which first foots might bring, in the east coast fishing communities this might well have been a herring. This custom somehow transplanted itself to Dundee in particular, where the fishy

117

token might even be dressed up with ribbons and lace and tied to the door of the visited house if the occupants were out. Symbolically attired or otherwise, this humble fish carried with it the token of prosperity.

Cakes and Cake Day

Food at New Year was also special and not just for its symbolic content. The tradition of rich fare, of shortbread and especially black bun (a rich fruit cake in a pastry crust), continues. Perhaps it has always had an incidental function: to soak up the quantities of liquid hospitality which have for so long been a part of the Scottish Hogmanay. Even so, the best of ingredients would be reserved for this most important occasion.

Walkers of Aberlour bake black bun, shortbread and Dundee Cake and thus remain in the mainstream of tradition, their quality fare an important part of the Scottish way of celebrating Hogmanay. However, some of the regional treats have been lost. In earlier times, special cakes were baked in St Andrews in Fife for its own version of Hogmanay called Cake Day. These cakes were given out to children by local shops, a practice certainly not confined to St Andrews. In fact, Scottish children would once have gone around the neighbourhood 'asking for their Hogmanay' from households and shops. In some places they dressed themselves in flowing sheets (perhaps echoing the Druids), which were then folded to form a large pocket or apron. As they went round the community they chanted Yuletide rhymes, such as the one on page 116, or:

> Ma feet's cauld, ma sheen's din,   shoes worn out
> gie's ma cakes and let's rin.   run

When the pocket on each apron was full the children went home, where the cakes proved a welcome bonus in many a poor household.

Often cakes were (and still are) baked at home as well. In the west of Scotland, for instance, an oat bannock was baked for each child in the family. These particular cakes were given a patterned edge and had a hole in the middle. They were also flavoured with caraway seeds. If any broke during the baking this was considered an ill omen for the child for whom it was intended. It is an interesting footnote to this now-extinct custom that the cake's wavy or patterned edge is also characteristic of shortbread rounds. Some say this is a symbol of the sun and is perhaps a curious echo of festive cakes baked for ceremonies or rituals connected with the sun worship of the Druids. Modified and handed down over so many generations, it can be difficult to interpret the original meanings – particularly as although the Druids held their rites in public their doctrines were secret and never written down.

Fire festivals

What can be made of the age-old tradition in Stonehaven, and elsewhere, of swinging fireballs in the streets at New Year? When midnight strikes,

the fireballs are lit and swung round and round by means of attached wires. Burghead, further along the coast from Stonehaven and facing the Moray Firth, varies the theme by holding its fire festival on 11th January – the old Hogmanay before the calendar was changed in 1600. The event is known as 'Burning of the Clavie' (the origin of this word is lost in obscurity). The Clavie King and his men carry a flaming half-barrel mounted on a pole along the streets of Burghead, following a traditional route. Finally the flaming barrel is taken to nearby Doorie Hill. (In former times each individual boat in the harbour was also visited by the Clavie. In 1875 it is recorded that a new vessel was named Doorie in a ceremony with the burning Clavie, which also involved the sprinkling of grain on her decks.) After the Clavie is fixed to the hilltop more fuel is added to the blaze, eventually leaving the dying embers which become sought after good luck charms, credited with bringing protection to the household for a year.

In Comrie, in Perthshire, another fire ceremony survives. Here the New Year is ushered in by the lighting of giant torches on large birch poles, which are then carried in procession about the town. The young men of Falkland in Fife still climb the East Lomond Hill with their torches. Flames of one sort or another were, and remain, a common feature of the Scots Hogmanay or New Year in many parts of the country. In spite of the Church trying to stamp out such pagan practices over the centuries, many hilltops used to be lit with bonfires to welcome in the New Year.

Every Hogmanay, this dramatic spectacle can be seen in the town of Stonehaven, south of Aberdeen. A fireball procession passes through the streets to frighten off evil spirits for the coming year; it ends with the fireballs being doused in the town's harbour.

119

Handsel Monday

Today, though some traditions have gone, the spirit of a new start with renewed friendship and contact with neighbours is still strong in Scotland. Gifts, especially of food, play an important part. Another aspect of the week-long yuletide festivities survived until quite recently: the celebration of Handsel Monday. This was the equivalent of England's Boxing Day, but took place on the first Monday of the New Year. Tradition demanded that presents should be given as tokens of goodwill, especially to servants or to anyone performing a service to the householder. This would even extend to giving extra feed to working animals. A curious variation on Handsel Monday which grew up in certain rural areas was that, although gift giving was duly observed, it was considered unlucky to handle money on Handsel Monday – which may have helped create the national stereotype of the thrifty Scot.

Although virtually forgotten now, Handsel Monday was another highlight in the otherwise 'dreich' (dull and miserable) days of January. How fortunate that Robert Burns was born on the 25th of the month, thereby giving the Scots cause for another celebration to keep them cheerful in the long nights. (Burns Suppers and the poet himself have already been described in Chapter Six.)

Up-Helly-Aa

It may not be a coincidence that Shetland, the most northerly part of Scotland, and where the nights are longest, squeezes in an extra deep-winter celebration. This is called Up-Helly-Aa and takes place on 29th January.

Up-Helly-Aa can be roughly taken to mean the end of the holidays – a reference to the end of the 24-day period in the old Viking festival of Jul. In common with other winter festivals, fire played an important part in this season. Until the 1870s, the men of Lerwick (the chief town of the islands) pulled burning tar barrels through the narrow streets of the town on primitive sleighs or stretchers at the end of this festival period. When the authorities became nervous about damage to property and outlawed the tar barrel, a torchlight procession was instigated. Then local pride in the islands' Norse past resulted in the introduction of a specially-made Viking galley in 1889. This made a spectacular show when burned and the 'tradition' has continued ever since.

The day of Up-Helly-Aa (which most Shetlanders consider the most important in the festive calendar) starts with the Jarl Squad, an elite group permitted to wear Viking costume, unveiling their hand-built galley. Separately, at the market cross in Lerwick (the islands' capital), a lengthy written discourse, known as 'the Bill', is displayed. The Jarl Squad spend the day visiting schools, hospitals and old folks homes, all the while showing un-Viking-like restraint and good behaviour. Then in the evening they lead the townsfolk for a torchlit march through the town, including groups of men in a variety of other costumes (including, so it is said, several in drag and quite a lot disguised as furry animals). The procession itself ends with the burning of the longship. However, this is far from the end of the evening, and for many it is when the fun really starts. Bands and musicians play in various halls all through the night. The troupes who appeared earlier in costume in the procession, and who have been in secret rehearsal for months beforehand, take turns to perform skits on local or international events. Strong drink is consumed and the whole night takes on the appearance of a particularly extrovert Scottish Hogmanay, though Shetland folk will insist there is no connection.

Gowkie Day

Just as the Presbyterian kirk (church) played down Christmas, so it ensured that north of the border neither was the Easter festival a very major event for the Scots. Easter Monday and, more especially, Good Friday, for example, are not necessarily taken as a holiday in Scotland. However, egg-rolling and other traditional (though not especially Scottish) activities can still be found. Meanwhile, Scotland's Auld Alliance partners, the French, are sometimes given the blame for introducing a strange custom in Scotland on 1st April. This used to be called Gowkie Day or 'Hunting the Gowk'. Generally a gowk in Scotland is a fool, but also more specifically, a cuckoo. As a cuckoo arriving in Scotland on 1st April would certainly be well ahead of schedule, it follows that hunting for one would be a very foolish pastime on that day. (To compound the odd association of 1st April and scarce Scottish cuckoos, the bird itself has various legends attached to it. The Scots used to think it was in league with the fairies and spent the winter in fairy hillocks.)

By way of Gowkie Day variations, Orkney used to have a Tailing Day on 2nd April. (Some say the tradition continues.) The object was to pin a tail to the coat of a victim. Perhaps totally unrelated, Orkney also celebrated Borrowing Day on 3rd April: a curious tradition that permitted any item borrowed on that day to be kept by the borrower. Not surprisingly, this potentially expensive custom barely survived into the twentieth century.

Beltane

While non-Celts marked the changing year with the solstices, hence the emphasis on deep midwinter, the Celts had two major marking points which divided the year. The first of these was May Day.

With their overtones of rebirth and the coming of the growing season, the fires which were once kindled on 1st May have very ancient origins, probably leading back to early sun worshipping. Early folk in Scotland sought favour from the god who gave them heat and light in a ceremony later called Beltane, perhaps from the name Baal, an eastern deity, and tein, a Celtic word meaning fire. Beltane practices of fire and sacrifices were at one stage the province of Druid priests. Folk memories of their rites, their true meanings lost long ago, survived until recent times and still found expression in festivals and celebrations. King James I of Scotland (1394–1437), while held captive by the English, wrote 'Kings Quair', a poem celebrating love and nature in the new season. In it he makes reference to a great May Day Fair held in Peebles in Scotland's Border country:

> At Beltane when ilke bodie bownis
> To Peblis to the play.
> To heir the singing and the soundis
> The solace suth to say.

Hill shepherds were among the last to give up the old Beltane fire ceremonies. Right into Victorian times in some places they would meet in a secret place on some high hillside. There a trench in the form of a ring – a symbol of the sun – would be cut. After various secret ceremonies a fire would be kindled within the ring on which a batter or caudle of eggs, butter, oatmeal and milk would be prepared. Thomas Pennant, the Welsh traveller who journeyed through Scotland in 1769, is commonly quoted. He describes how the shepherds, having built the fire and made the caudle – and no doubt having partaken of the copious supplies of beer and whisky which were a necessary part of the gathering – began by spilling some of the eggy mixture on the ground as a libation. Next, everyone present took an oatcake which had been specially baked with nine raised knobs or squares upon it. These nine squares were broken off one at a time and dedicated either to a protector of or predator upon the flocks. The shepherd faced the fire and flung a piece of oatcake over his shoulder saying 'This I give to thee, preserve thou my horses; this to thee, preserve thou my sheep', and so on. Then the predators were acknowledged: 'This I give to thee, o fox, spare thou my lambs' – and the ceremony continued with offerings to hooded crow, eagle and anything else which affected the sheep's wellbeing. Afterwards, the company feasted upon the caudle – except that Pennant and others noted that the remains of the food were hidden for other herdsmen to turn up on the following Sunday and finish off.

Around the basic element of a hilltop fire there were variations. Sometimes all of the company leapt through the 'purifying' flames. Or lots would be drawn (perhaps by selecting the one blackened piece from a broken bannock) to see who would leap the fire three times. This has the slightly sinister echo of lots originally drawn for human sacrifice. Other accounts describe the building of two fires so that cattle could be symbolically driven between them.

A curious link between Easter and Beltane is noted by Pennant, who describes how in some places:

> a cross is cut in some sticks which is then dipped in pottage and the Thursday before Easter one of each is placed over the sheep-cot, the stable, or the cow-house. On the 1st of May they are carried to the hill where the rites are celebrated, all decked with wild flowers, and after the feast is over, replaced over the spots they were taken from; and this was originally styled Clou-an-Beltein, or the split branch of the fire of the rock.

He ends with the sharply dismissive observation:

> These follies are now seldom practiced, and that with the utmost secrecy; for the Clergy are indefatigable in discouraging every species of superstition.

This cross symbol occurs again in an interesting but now lost tradition in Badenoch on Speyside. On Beltane morning, specially baked oatcakes, marked on one side with a cross and on the other with a circle, were rolled down the hillside. The rolling of round bannocks with cross marks was practised in other parts of the country as well. This introduction of a Christian symbol into a practice which is probably pagan in origin is just one small-scale example of the tendency for the early church to graft Christian ritual on to pagan celebrations – hence Yule became the Feast of the Nativity.

The Beltane fires were also carried down the hill to rekindle the fires at home, the intention being to keep the flame burning all year. This fire, in its domestic context, was significant enough to demand its own rituals throughout the year, particularly that of 'smoorin' (smothering) or subduing the fire to smouldering point, to enable it to stay in all night. In a mix of church sentiment and pagan ritual, the embers in Highland homes were each night spread out on the hearth – which in former times would have been in the middle of the floor – and made into a circle. This was then made into three equal sections with a boss left in the centre. Three peats were laid to touch the boss. The first was laid in the name of the God of Life, the second to the God of Peace and the third to the God of Grace. The ashes were then heaped in the centre, while the 'Three of Light' was invoked. This raised heap was called the Tula NanTri (Hearth of the Three). Finally, any one of a number of invocations or formulae would be recited:

Smaladh an Teine	**Smoorin the Fire**
An Tri numh	The sacred Three
A chumhnadh,	To save,
A chomhnadh,	To shield,
A chomraig,	To surround,
A tula,	The hearth,
An taighe,	The house,

123

Am taghlaich,	The household,
An oidhche,	This eve,
An nochd,	This night,
O an oidhche,	O this eve,
An nochd,	This night,
Agus gach oidhche,	And every night,
Gach aon oidhche.	Each single night.
Amen	Amen

It should be remembered that May Day once also had a practical significance. In the Highlands it was the day when the move was made from winter quarters in the glen to summer sheilings on the high hill pastures. In the days when the Highlanders had a cattle-based local economy, those black and wiry beasts were driven alpine-style to the new spring grass. The women and children went along as well to tend the beasts and make butter and cheese. In the glen below the men could then tend crops without hindrance from straying cattle. This flit (household move) was helped by the menfolk, who carried up some of the heavier domestic implements, but the day was made special by the feasting upon new season's lamb, with prayers said for the protection of the livestock (and probably the women and children as well!). This special feast is perhaps a link with the May Day sacrifices of ancient times.

Nowadays only faint traces of various forms of Beltane ceremonies survive. One is the tradition of washing in the May Day dew of dawn, a custom still observed by many local Edinburgh folk who make their way up Arthur's Seat, the city's own mini-mountain. This washing is said to beautify a maiden's complexion, as May Day dew was highly regarded as a potent and magical fluid by the Druids. The washing in dew may even be linked to some kind of anointing prior to sacrifice. Ben Ledi near Callander, Kinnoull Hill by Perth and Tinto Hill near Lanark sometimes also have May Day congregations, and the path up to Ben Ledi can be extremely busy on Midsummer Eve as well – perhaps indicating the lingering of a folk memory still associated with these once sacred spots, which were clearly visited more than once in the course of the pagan festive calendar.

While almost all significance of May Day has vanished in the bustle of modern Scotland, one other tiny reminder survives. Fittingly it is observed in a certain long and comparatively remote glen in the heart of Perthshire. Today this glen has all the typical ingredients of the twentieth-century Highlands: forestry and sheep grazing, a 'big hoose' tucked behind a high wall, and a great dam in the upper part of the glen supplying hydroelectric power. But beyond the paraphernalia of the present, across a waste of heather and grassland, lonely and open to the winds, there can still be found the Tigh Nam Bodach (house of the old men). Only a few feet high and round, it is made of stones without mortar. At some ancient time the folk of the glen built it as a shrine to the elemental forces of the seasons. Inside, they believed, dwelt the spirit of the Cailleach (Gaelic for

old woman, though in this case more particularly the Earth Mother, the giver of life). The spirit is personified by a worn stone, less than knee-high, vaguely shaped like a squat figure. Beside it is another, smaller stone of similar shape. This is the Bodach (Gaelic meaning the old man). Beside them are some much smaller stones. This little family in stone spend the winter inside the closed off house. Yet every spring a local hillman strides the long miles to take out the stones, spreading them on the new grass so that they can enjoy the new season. Each autumn they are as reverently put back into their shrine. Thus in the middle of modern Scotland, at least one community is keeping a very ancient tradition alive and marking the endless turning of the seasons in the manner of the early folk.

Midsummer

After Beltane, the traditional calendar runs on to Midsummer. For the Celtic people of Scotland this was less important than the time of sowing, around Beltane or May Day, and of reaping or summer's end, formerly called Samhainn or Hallowmass, on 1st November; but there has been some merging of the faint traces of tradition which remain, with folk still gathering on hilltops to witness the midsummer dawn. However, the midsummer light is strong and, in the north, almost endless, while grass is usually in plentiful supply for flocks and herds. The need to bring fire into the darkness was less strong, the urge to propitiate any deity less compelling.

Samhainn

However, at the end of summer, another mark was made in the turning season. The ancient Celts called it Samhainn, the fire of Baal, celebrated at the end of the growing season. Just as Beltane symbolised the beginning of life in the new season, so Samhainn was involved with death and endings. Christian practice grafted on its own ceremony of Hallowmass or All Saints' Day. All over Europe in this season it was also believed that the souls of the departed revisited their former haunts.

The surviving traditional activities of Hallowe'en, the 31st October, which still exist in Scotland today thus have a variety of elements. Strands of an ancient Celtic festival overlaid with early Christian beliefs can be recognised by folklorists, but added to this are the practices associated with the Europe-wide cult of witchcraft. In fact, until mid-Victorian times, in some parts of Scotland fires were still kindled on hilltops. Even Queen Victoria enjoyed the annual Hallowe'en activities at Balmoral Castle on Deeside, which involved the burning of a witch effigy on top of a bonfire

125

amid dancing, piping and the consumption of plenty of drams of whisky.

However, gradually the focus moved indoors with the celebration evolving into a variety of games and jollities. This was true on both sides of the border. Perhaps the best-known game, and probably still just surviving, is 'dookin' (ducking) for apples.

To the ancient Celts, apples were talismans which enabled the bearer to enter the Land of the Immortals, sometimes called Avalon or Apple-Hall – a place which could only be reached after crossing water. Thus the combined elements of apple and water survive even in today's ducking ceremonies. The participant gains apples (or immortality) only by going through water. In long-forgotten Druid practice, an apple was also a symbol of augury and this belief in the role of apples in foretelling the future survived long after the secrets of the Druids were lost. In the traditional ballad of Thomas the Rhymer, who was one of the most famous of Scotland's seers, an apple is a great gift:

> Syne they came to a garden green   then
> And she pu'd an apple frae a tree
> 'Tak this for thy wages, True Thomas,
> It will give the tongue that will never lie'

The apple kept its mystique down through the long ages until very recent times. A widespread former Hallowe'en custom was for a girl to peel an apple in a continuous ribbon. She would then throw the peel over her shoulder and it would fall into the shape of the initial letter of her future partner's name. (This is now believed to be an echo of the old Druid rites of foretelling the future by the agonised twists and writhing of the sacrificial victim.) Lowland Scotland had its own variation on the theme of association of apple and future partner. A girl eating an apple while combing her hair at midnight on Hallowe'en could, after throwing a piece of apple over her shoulder, see the image of her future partner in a mirror placed before her, if she looked through the veil formed by her hair.

Some former Hallowe'en customs in Scotland were certainly bizarre. There existed, for example, the faintly dubious practice of partners seeking to know each other's future by using kale or cabbage stalks as a means of divination. This involved entering a spinster's or bachelor's garden, hand in hand and with eyes shut, and pulling up one stalk of cabbage or kale. This was then examined. If the stalk was strong and healthy, then the future spouse would be 'well formed in person and purse', as the folklorist puts it. If no earth clung to the roots, the couple's future would be poverty-stricken. Even the temper of the partner could be gauged by biting the stalk to ascertain the degree of sweetness or sourness.

Another formerly common practice was to use hazelnuts to foretell the likely course of a relationship between a couple. Amid much hilarity, pairs of nuts would be suitably named after likely combinations of partners and placed close to the fire. How the nuts reacted to the heat would indicate the course of the relationship: if they burned quietly together that indicated harmony; if they popped or shot apart this suggested a stormy future.

126

Hazel trees growing in Scotland were habitually pillaged just before Hallowe'en to provide 'ammunition' for this entertainment. At first sight it seems an odd custom, but must surely echo ancient lore. The hazel was a magic tree to the Celts, regarded as the source and symbol of wisdom. The white wand of the Druid priest was originally a hazel wand, stripped of its bark.

Throwing the clue (or clew), meaning a ball of yarn, was another method of foretelling future partners – clearly a preoccupation at Hallowe'en, with the long winter nights ahead. The method was simple. The woman who wished to have this knowledge found her nearest lime-kiln and threw in a clue of freshly wound blue yarn, while holding on to one end. She then asked who held the other. The name was uttered from the sepulchral depths of the kiln. This practice had a further advantage in that a quick-witted and ardent youth could lurk in advance in the lime-kiln and hence influence the result. Perhaps lime-kilns were substituted for ancient burial sites and the echo of voices beyond the grave.

In fact, Hallowe'en gave many opportunities for tinkering with fate, especially when it came to choosing partners. These include the midnight practice of sowing hemp seed while incanting: 'Hemp seed I sow thee, hemp seed I sow thee and he who is my true love come behind and harrow

Once the main drawing power on farms all over Scotland, the horse and master worked as a team. In places, this mysterious relationship between horse and man was embodied in 'The Horseman's Word', part-folklore, part-secret society, which seemed to give those with inside knowledge a power over the farm beasts.

127

thee'. This obviously enabled any suitors in the vicinity (who were not hovering hopefully in dusty lime-kilns) to appear in the darkness.

Similar opportunities presented themselves in the practice of measuring bere-stacks, that is, stacks made with bere, a primitive or early species of barley. The midnight ploy was to walk three times round the stack, arms outstretched as if measuring it. On the third revolution, the seeker of the future could clasp in her arms the image of her future partner. In the darkness of a cold autumn night in a farm stackyard it is not hard to imagine how easily such a shade might become reality. The use of cabbage stalks or barley is also a reminder that certain types of augury in Druidic practice centred round the fruits of the harvest.

Evidence that these traditions and several more were actively practised can be found in Robert Burns' poem 'Hallowe'en', which describes one riotous occasion where the assembled company tries many tests. The outdoor games cause much confusion in the darkness while the indoor ones have plenty of merriment. However, in another of Burns' poems, 'Tam Glen', the lad who gives his name to the title is more seriously in the thoughts of a lass who has tried yet another Hallowe'en custom:

The last Hallowe'en I was waukin	awake
My droukit sark-sleeve as ye ken	soaking wet shirt-sleeve
His likeness cam up the house staukin	walking stealthily
And the very grey breeks o Tam Glen!	breeches or trousers

The lass is lying awake awaiting the image of her intended to pass before her. She has followed the recipe for this method of divination by finding a south-running spring or burn at the meeting point of three lairds' lands. There she has dipped her left shirt-sleeve in the water because it was believed that if the shirt was placed to dry before a fire and the wearer lay down nearby, the shade of her future partner would be seen just before midnight turning the sleeve over as if to dry it.

What survives even in written form about past practices at Hallowe'en is clearly very ancient, with fire, fertility ritual, and perhaps even hallucinogenic practices with hemp, overlaid with Christian sentiment. However, traditions move on, blending and changing with time. The customs of Hallowe'en in more modern times have also involved dressing up in costume. In Scotland, the wearer of the masquerade is known as a guiser (pronounced guyser almost to rhyme with miser and probably cognate with English geezer). This word has already been mentioned in connection with Shetland's Up-Helly-Aa which certainly involves a lot of dressing up. As for the masks which are a traditional part of the costume, some say the masked folk are simply symbolic of the spirits who are abroad on that evening, while others say the guisers are masked to avoid being recognised by the spirits. As a further possibility, the masks can also be seen as symbols of the whole range of bogles, beasties, banshees and whigmaleeries and other outrageous denizens of the Scottish rural imagination created by witchcraft or traditional beliefs.

In recent years, Hallowe'en entertainment in Scotland has survived in many places, though mainly consisting of parties of children, mostly in costume and usually with turnip lanterns (symbolic skulls – another reminder that Samhainn was bound up with the dead), who knock on doors and offer minimal entertainment to secure a contribution to their fireworks fund with the incantation 'penny for the guy'. In Scotland, Hallowe'en rites and ceremonies remained particularly vigorous right down from Druidic times until the comparatively recent confusion of Guy (as in Fawkes) with guising or dressing up at Hallowe'en. Thus Scotland's own tradition has become blended with the much younger and purely English business on 5th November of celebrating the failure of Guy Fawkes who tried to blow up England's Parliament in 1605 – a feat to which many Scots would have given their blessing.

Annual farming celebrations

If Yule, Beltane and Hallowe'en were some of the fixed dates in the festival year, to some extent acknowledged by town and country folk alike and even crossing barriers of class, there were other markers in the year of special interest to farming communities in particular. The 28th May and 28th November were the key dates before which hiring fairs or feein markets were held in rural areas right across Scotland. There, farmhands would seek work, contracting for a six-month term. These gatherings in market towns were boisterous affairs, where the men would be on a spree in the market square and in the surrounding places of refreshment.

In addition to the feein markets, there was also a huge number of fair days, originally linked to saints' days when the monks sold their produce as part of the holy festival. These fairs may have reached their peak in the eighteenth century. A few even survive, though their role as a place of horse-dealing and trading between town and country folk has long been eclipsed by the fairground and side-show ambience which prevails today. Aikey Fair, near Old Deer in Aberdeenshire and held in late July, was formerly an event with an awesome reputation, discussed in hushed tones by the 'douce' (Scots for sober and respectable) God-fearing townsfolk. St Andrews and Kirkcaldy in Fife, further south, still have fairground attractions marking the times of these ancient fairs. However, most are just a faint memory, including the Timmer Market in Aberdeen in August. Its speciality was the sale of 'timmer' (timber, i.e. wooden) implements, such as 'coggies' (bowls), 'spurtles' (wooden stirring spoons) and creepie stools, used by children to creep in close to the fire.

Amongst this former wealth of fairs, there was even one held overnight, appropriately called Sleepy Market. This dusk to dawn fair was held in the Garioch, a part of Aberdeenshire. Only after the unsettled times of 1746 (the year of Culloden) was it turned into a day fair. Nowadays, the horse dealers, the pedlars, the sellers of tracts and chapbooks, the entertainers,

the ale-wives, and the stalls with their excitement and colour have gone from here as from almost everywhere else. Only an echo remains in the local farm name: Sleepytown.

Other celebrations helped ease the 'tyauve' (Scots for hard work or struggle) of the farming year. Till well into the nineteenth century, Fastern's E'en (Shrove Tuesday) was one notable day in the rural calendar because meat was served to the farming crew. This was sometimes known as a 'beef, brose and bannock day'. The brose, as related in Chapter Seven, was all too usual, but the combination with beef and bannocks signified a special occasion. This early year feast gradually died away and was in any case less important than celebrations revolving round a successful harvest.

No matter how niggardly the farmer in his year-round provision to his farmhands, both they and the visiting band of harvesters were usually well fed as they took in the crop. Later, the real celebrations took place when all was safely gathered. However, even before that, the cutting of the last sheaf had its own special significance. In some places, the shearers threw their sickle at the standing corn, in a curious ritual to avoid the blame associated with the last cut. Also in parts of the Highlands, the last sheaf would be dressed to resemble a woman in cap, frock, shawl and apron. Sometimes this went further and the sheaf would have in 'her' apron some bread and cheese and at the waistband a hand sickle, thus making the effigy into a female shearer. Sometimes she was the Maiden, sometimes the Cailleach (Gaelic for old woman). Usually she had the honour of being placed at the head of the table at the harvest supper which marked the last of the cutting. Sometimes she was swept off her feet into the dance which followed, before being tossed aside as a bite for the horses later in the year.

If that was the broad Highland format, then the Lowlanders differed only in detail. The Gaelic Cailleach became the Scots 'clyack' and the cutting of the clyack-sheaf was an honour rather than a task to be avoided. It was likewise decorated, at least with ribbons. Usually it was kept till Old Yule, then was fed to the birds, or the farm beasts. In some places, this symbol of a plentiful harvest was set above the door of the farm, or over the farmer's bed, or wherever its good luck was considered most useful.

In short, there was a host of rituals associated with the cutting of the last of the corn. However, the greatest of the celebrations in Scotland's farming year was reserved for the time when all of the harvest was safely under cover in the stackyard. Then the barn would be tidied for the farmtoun's 'meal-and-ale'. This was basically a harvest supper, a down-to-earth celebration. Its centrepiece was a dish (the meal-and-ale itself) of some potency, with all of the basic ingredients used in Scotland's ancient ceremonies: chiefly oatmeal and strong drink. Thus oats, beer, whisky and syrup or sugar would be stirred in together. (There may have been other ingredients, but the recipes were closely guarded secrets.) Also into the dish went ancient symbols or charms such as silver coins, rings, buttons and other talismans. This brew was set in its own large dish in the table

Opposite: In former times, ploughing competitions between horse-drawn teams were widespread in Scotland. In South Ronaldsay on Orkney, the local children copied their seniors and ploughed on the sands. This has gradually evolved into an annual event known as the Boys Ploughing Match. Miniature ploughs are used and the children are dressed in ornate costumes.

centre and was supped communally. Those who found a ring were likely to get partners in the near future, while those who found the button in their spoon were not to be favoured. The finders of the silver coins, usually sixpences, had the most immediate reward from fate.

Perhaps to counteract the heady effect of the meal-and-ale, a substantial main course of meat was then served, with – perhaps most special of all – a clootie dumpling to follow. (This is basically a rich steamed pudding boiled in a cloth and is traditional festive fare.) There might follow toasts and thanks to the harvest crew and the neighbours, and then the tables would be cleared for dancing. Several meal-and-ales would happen in a farming district around the same time, and the pagan gods were thus propitiated for another year.

Finally, when the celebrations were over, late in the season the feast of Thanksgiving Sunday would be soberly held in the local kirk, and a liberal splashing of the freezing waters of Calvinism would perhaps temporarily douse the flames of ancient festivities.

The Horseman's Word

There were darker elements in the farming world, particularly in the rituals once associated with the ploughman and his horse. Wherever the sturdy Clydesdale horses were harnessed to ploughs to struggle against the stony earth, the men whose job it was to look after this power resource on the farm were like a race apart. Hence the wealth of songs and traditional tales about ploughmen.

One of the most curious elements was the awe and mystique attached to those who had undergone the rites and had the secret of 'The Horseman's Word' (sometimes the horseman's grippin word). This gave the initiated power to command the beasts he worked, as well as power over women around the farm. Having its origins, some say, in a Dark Ages cult, the secrets of the horseman's craft were passed on at the dead of night in curious rituals and practices which at one time were observed throughout much of Scotland and over the border too. Its headquarters were in the north-east where farm cottages and accommodation tended to be grouped around the main farm (hence farmtoun) which could be quite isolated. In this the north-east differed from the English practice of agricultural labourers tending to live in villages away from the farms themselves.

The ceremony involved taking young farmhands, who wished to become ploughmen, blindfolded to a barn on the farm at the dead of night. The organisers of the ceremony would already be inside. There followed a series of ritual questions and answers, with the initiates stripped naked in front of an altar made up of a bushel measure inverted on top of a sack of grain. Blindfolded and confused and subjected to tests of secrecy as well as much whisky drinking, the ceremony must have been an ordeal for many a young man. In addition, those undergoing the ceremony were taken into the recesses of the barn where they met a shaggy horned figure

132

whose cloven hoof they shook. Only after that did the foreman whisper the word to them.

The farmers, it is to be noted, took absolutely no part in these ceremonies and they even attempted to stop them, because after initiation the new horseman was given his own pair of horses and the farmer was told that he would have to pay the 'boy' a man's wages.

This above ceremony was only a stage in the learning of the lore of horses, some of which has now been lost. Some of it concerned know-ledge, for instance, of which scents a horse would tolerate. To an outsider, even a farmer unaware of the insiders' knowledge, the sight of a horseman calming a horse simply by whispering something in its ear was certainly magical – even if it went unnoticed that with his other hand the horseman might, for example, be holding a repellant or calming substance below the horse's nostrils. Drugs and potions were certainly an integral part of the knowledge which went along with the Horseman's Word. Some claim it was akin to witchcraft, while others see it as close to Freemasonry, a secret society with various levels of knowledge. A few believe that, like witch-craft, it has not died out and clings on in a few out-of-the-way places. As for the word itself, a few published accounts have made guesses, but to respect tradition it is best not to enquire too closely.

The Boys Ploughing Match

Though the team of man and horse has ceased to be important on Scot-land's farms, tradition has been maintained in a unique festival which celebrates the ploughman's role. The Boys Ploughing Match or Festival of the Horse takes place on the third Saturday in August in the village of St Margaret's Hope in South Ronaldsay, Orkney.

In the days when horses drew the plough, there were ploughing com-petitions in many parts of Scotland between the various farm crews. These still take place, although the ploughs are now drawn by tractors. On South Ronaldsay, the youngsters copied their seniors and ploughed for fun, along the sands or on the waste corner of a field, using makeshift ploughs and their younger brothers or sisters as horses. This is thought to have evolved in the early years of the nineteenth century. Eventually these mini-ploughing matches became more formalised with each district tak-ing its youngsters' match quite seriously. Today this has developed further, the ploughs being exactly miniaturised metal ploughs and the children dressed in ornate decorated horse harnesses.

The event is now held at peak holiday time, giving many visitors a chance to see this unique celebration; both the judging of costume and the actual ploughing on smooth sand of perfect furrows in tiny 'fields' about 4 foot square. Prizes are awarded, then everyone has a party and this slice of rural life is kept alive for another year.

 NINE

SUPERSTITIONS AND MYTHICAL BEASTS

Highland landscapes are full of enchantment – not in the sense that this word is often used in modern tourist brochures, but with a hint of something older and deeper. Strange happenings are said to have befallen visitors here. Could it be that the land really is haunted?

One recent visitor related how, while walking alone in the wild lands between the Coulin and Ben Damph forests south of Glen Torridon in Wester Ross, he suddenly felt chilled, and was brought to a standstill by the unexpected and eerie sound of nearby children's laughter. He was miles from any road, with a steep hillside on one side of him and rolling moors on the other. Rooted to the spot, he could hear only the ripple of water at his feet. The laughter did not sound again, but so unsettled was the visitor by this strange episode, that he felt obliged to return to the main glen by the shortest route possible.

A personal experience involved a frightening night's camping in Sutherland. This was some years ago, in my student days. For some inexplicable reason, the campsite chosen, in a hollow, out of sight of a nearby minor road which led down to the ferry departure point for Handa island, became so completely oppressive and unbearable that my companion and I, in some state of panic, dismantled the tent at midnight and spent the night in the car in a layby some miles away! Some time later, I learned of a murder that had been committed not so very far from the area, many years earlier, and of strange apparitions which had been seen there since . . .

Opposite: There was a widespread belief in Scotland that the wood of the rowan tree would protect the household against witches and it was often planted near the door of crofts or other rural dwellings. This example is near Applecross in Wester Ross.

Rowans and strange rites

What makes the Highland background of these stories so fascinating? After all, many folk have some kind of paranormal experience at one time or another, and most have no Highland connection whatsoever. Yet something persists. Perhaps it is an echo of emptiness, a reminder of past dramas still flitting around tumbled stones of now deserted summer sheilings, where the guardian rowan tree grows.

134

It is widely held that the rowan tree keeps witches away, and a rowan at the door of the croft was often thought to protect the family within. Specific items of household equipment would be made from rowan wood for the same reason: the staff used to agitate the churn in butter-making, or the pin to the shackle which kept the cows still while milking. In fact, the practice of growing rowan was not even entirely confined to the Highlands. In Lowland areas, as well, the tree was considered lucky and planted accordingly, sometimes to create an archway, in the way that it once was trained over the byre door or the entrance to the cow yard.

Wishing wells and wishing trees

Even in comparatively recent times, trees – and certainly not only rowans – which have been growing near certain sacred spots, such as springs or wells, seem to have taken on a special mystique and have become wishing trees. One of the most famous is an oak tree on Isle Maree, one of the smaller of the islands on Loch Maree in Wester Ross – often reckoned to be one of the most beautiful lochs in Scotland. Originally this ancient tree played its part in healing rites connected to an equally venerable well on the little island. However, by the time the spot had been visited by Queen Victoria in 1877, the ceremony had been reduced to fixing or hammering a metal object, usually a coin, into the poor tree, while silently making a wish. In Loch Maree's case, any healing was specifically for insanity. In its heyday many centuries ago, the tradition involved rowing the patient around the little island and dipping him at least three times in the loch. Eventually brought to land, the now dripping sufferer would kneel before a rude altar and then drink 'holy water' from the well, before an offering was attached to the aforementioned tree.

Prior to that time, some say as late as the seventeenth century, the island had been the scene of much sacrificing of bulls. To the pre-Christians, bulls were sacred creatures, their curved horns thought to resemble the crescent moon. In one of its variants the moon deity was named Ur in Celtic speech. The name then became Mo-Urie or Mourie, which was later confused with Maol Rubha, the name of an Irish monk (640–722) who came to the island. A ruined chapel, successor to this saint's hermitage, can still be seen on the island. This is a good example of the weaving together of traditions and their gradual change and evolution through time. In this case a link between prim Victoriana and pre-Christian animal sacrifices via moon worship and a cure for lunacy! At one time, there were literally hundreds of sacred wells in Scotland – the symbol of birth and beginning is clearly a very ancient one.

Another famous example of a sacred spot associated with water, though more specifically a river pool rather than a well, is in Strath Fillan, between Crianlarich and Tyndrum in the central Highlands. The strath is named after a certain St Fillan who came from Ireland during the seventh century.

Now visible from a new road bridge which runs straight through the

valley is a section of the River Fillan traditionally called Linnhe Naoimh or the Holy Pool. For centuries this spot drew pilgrims because of its supposed miraculous healing powers associated with the saint. The healing rites here are well documented – especially since the extraordinary practice took place as recently as 1860.

The best time for healing was during the moon's first quarter. Men and women bathed in the Holy Pool, and each had to find nine small stones from the rocky river bed. Having found the right number, those seeking to be cured took the stones to three cairns which stood on raised land nearby. They circled each cairn three times, placing a single stone on the cairn after each circuit. Then a piece of clothing, which would normally cover the part of the body which required healing, was likewise placed on the cairn, along with some silver as a token of faith. The cure would then be effected.

Even more bizarre was a healing ritual for the insane. This took place on the chapel site. First the sufferer, attached only by a halter, was flung into the Holy Pool, then retrieved and taken to the chapel where he or she was tied to a special wicker frame. It was important that the patient's head was placed inside the font. Straw was then used to cover the victim and St Fillan's magic bell was placed on his or her forehead. The sufferer was left all night in this position. If by morning the bindings or straps had been loosened, the patient was declared cured. If not, the whole ritual was repeated a month later!

Rob Roy MacGregor once showed an impressive lack of reverence for these rites when he performed a similar ceremony on a Campbell land agent whom he felt had illegally evicted a MacGregor family in Glen Dochart. After 'persuading' him to renew the MacGregor lease, Rob decided to 'cure' the agent's apparent lunacy by giving him the ducking treatment, after which he left the dripping unfortunate strapped to the frame in the churchyard.

The tradition of visiting sacred wells has all but died out. A few still visit Tobar Na h'Oige (the well of youth) in a birch wood near Culloden House, Inverness, though as recently as the 1930s special buses were laid on from Inverness on the first Sunday in May. The well here was given a Christian flavour by the name St Mary's Well, but it is also called the Cloutie Well, from the clouts or strips of cloth hung on the bushes nearby by pilgrims. Other once-famous sites are now virtually forgotten. St Baodan's Well falls in this category. The site exists close to Ardchattan Priory, the second-oldest continually occupied house in Scotland, founded in 1231. St Baodan was an early Celtic saint who had a cell here. In an effort to supplant the old pre-Christian practices and convert communities, early holy men frequently took up residence close to sacred sites.

Another deserted sacred well is the Loch Seunta Well, named after the adjacent secluded loch in the north of Skye. The Skye-born traveller Martin Martin, in *A Description of the Western Islands of Scotland* (1703), describes it as a well whose curative properties were well known as a 'specifick for several diseases such as stitches, headaches, stone,

137

consumptions, megrim'. The cure involved a familiar procedure: three times sun-wise round the well, a draught of its water, and a small offering. While Martin's list of cures from this well is quite wide-ranging, some wells were extremely specific. For instance, around Kenmore, at the east end of Loch Tay in Perthshire, were two wells: one for toothache and the other for sore eyes. Others were specific for measles or whooping cough.

The tradition of visiting wells persisted until the early years of this century. Perhaps the leaching of minerals from nearby rocks did have curative powers, but in today's technological age, where the word of medical science is often held as sacred as the words of the early saints once were, such lore is now lost.

Witches and seers

The holders of specialist knowledge, and thus the conveyers of tradition, have always been slightly set apart from the rest of society. Sometimes in the past awe of the wise one became suspicion, and then suspicion mixed with fear, leading to wild accusations of witchcraft. Scotland was certainly not exempt from this, particularly during the sixteenth and seventeenth centuries. Indeed, by the seventeenth century, cases of witchcraft were hardly even mentioned in court records, so common had they become. One estimate suggests that between 1479 and 1722 over 17,000 individuals – mostly women – were tortured and executed in Scotland alone. Executing witches proved a profitable recreation for government officials because the estate of anyone so accused became the property of the Crown.

From such singular unpleasantness, it is a relief to turn to those legendary witches often associated with Scotland's landscape. One famous witch is the Cailleach Bheur, associated with a number of hills including Ben Nevis. According to legend, she once kept a beautiful maiden prisoner there. However, her malice was undone by her son, who fell in love with the girl and escaped with her, in spite of the witch brewing up fearful storms – a not uncommon happening on the Ben. The Cailleach was also active on Schiehallion in Perthshire, where a feature called Sgriob na Cailleach, or the old woman's furrow, is named after her. Westwards, Loch Awe in Argyll was also her responsibility. High on Ben Cruachan, which overlooks the loch to the north, she had the task, according to tradition, of uncovering a spring each morning by rolling back a huge boulder, and stopping it at night by rolling it forward again. Very tired one evening, she dozed off and forgot to stop up the spring. The overflowing waters that resulted were sufficient to form Loch Awe.

Thomas the Rhymer

A talent once strongly associated with the Highlands, and not just with witches, was 'second sight', or the ability to see the future. However, this talent was not confined solely to the folk in the Highlands. The thirteenth-century Laird of Ercildoune, Thomas Learmont, better known as Thomas the Rhymer, was certainly a real eccentric, but one who attracted a number of extraordinary tales. Legend has it that after an encounter with the Queen of the Fairies, he was taken into Fairyland and there acquired the gift of prophecy. The ballad of Thomas the Rhymer sets the scene:

> True Thomas lay on Huntlie bank;
> A ferlie he spied wi his ee;   sight/eye
> For there he saw a lady bright
> Come riding down by the Eildon Tree

After this seven-year vacation with the 'queen of fair Elfland', Thomas came back and was eventually 'rehabilitated' in the neighbourhood.

The Eildon Hills in the Scottish Borders are associated with Thomas the Rhymer, thirteenth-century seer and poet who met with the Queen of Elfland and was spirited away. While in Elfland he acquired his gifts of prophecy.

139

Naturally, his neighbours were at first suspicious of his reappearance. However, after several of his prophecies came true, he became an adviser to the king. One of the prophecies made by True Thomas was the extinction of the Learmont line:

> The hare sall kittle on my hearth-stane,   litter
> and there will never be a laird Learmont again

According to eye witnesses, in 1839 a hare was seen in the now derelict Rhymer's Tower, once the family seat. Sure enough, two leverets were found behind a nettle bush growing in the fireplace.

On another occasion, Thomas predicted the continuing welfare of the Haigs at Bemersyde, a house which the family still occupy to this day. Perhaps the best-known member of this family was Douglas, first Earl Haig of Bemersyde (1861–1928).

> Tyde what may
> Whatere betyde
> Haig shall be Haig
> of Bemersyde

The Lady of Lawers

Another well-known set of traditions is associated with the seer known as Baintighearna Labhuir, or the Lady of Lawers. She lived in the seventeenth century and seemed to specialise in bold and unambiguous predictions. So far, all but three have come true in every detail, with the last fulfilment as recent as 1948. She is thought to have been a Stewart of Appin who came east as a bride to the parish of Lawers on the north side of Loch Tay in Perthshire. She lived in the old village of Lawers, now a roofless collection of ruins in woodlands by the loch side. Her predictions were made in written form in a contemporary manuscript kept for years in Taymouth Castle but now lost. However, they were also recorded orally, and these transmissions were set down in print during the last century.

Some prophecies were of a local nature but nevertheless pointed to economic conditions then in the future. 'There will be a mill on every burn and a plough in every field and the two sides of Loch Tay will become a kale garden.' In time the lands fell into the hands of the powerful Marquises of Breadalbane who introduced flax growing and milling as part of their improvement schemes in the eighteenth century. These lint mills were the first seen in the Highlands and were water-powered, using the burns running down to the loch. Likewise the improvements brought enclosures and much more intensive ploughing and cultivation, hence fulfilling the kale garden part of the prophecy. The Lady of Lawers also saw the coming of the Clearances in her prediction 'the land will first be sifted, then riddled of its people'. The second Marquis of Breadalbane evicted at least 500 families from 1834 onwards, so that a population that once stood at 3,500 around the loch at the start of the nineteenth century,

is today still only a little over a hundred. 'The jaw of the sheep will drive the plough from the ground' indicated that the fairly intensive agriculture would give way to lands used only for sheep grazing – true today as any traveller along the loch can see.

The Lady also made a whole series of predictions about the fate of the Campbells of Glenorchy, who became the Earls and Marquises of Breadalbane and rose to hold the biggest estate in Scotland. At one time this stretched from Loch Tay to the Atlantic. In the present century, however, all of this estate has been split or otherwise sold. 'The last Laird will pass over Glenogle with a grey pony leaving nothing behind.' Sure enough, when the last property, Kinnell House, at Killin was sold in 1948, the last Laird, the ninth Earl of Breadalbane, left Killin and took the train southwards over Glenogle. Accompanying him was a small grey pony which many saw loaded onto the train.

As for the Lady's unfulfilled prophecies, one is obscure; the second, however, predicted that a ship 'driven by smoke' will sink in Loch Tay with loss of life. Pleasure steamers plied the loch until 1939, though it is said that their trade was depressed with the fairly common knowledge of the prophecy. It seems unlikely that the steamer service will now be resurrected. The third is the most intriguing. 'The time will come when Ben Lawers will become so cold that it will chill and waste the land for seven miles around it.' Now a National Trust for Scotland property, Ben Lawers, at 1,214 m (3,984 ft) is the highest hill in Perthshire and seems benign enough. But as plenty of the other unlikely predictions of the Lady of Lawers have come true, who knows what the future holds, in spite of global warming?

The Brahan Seer

Perhaps the most famous series of Highland prophecies were made by the Brahan Seer. Brahan (pronounced braan) is the name of an estate about four miles south-west of Dingwall in Easter Ross. He was a man called Coinneach Odhar (pronounced Co-in-yach Ore meaning, in Gaelic, Brown Kenneth). Though a Lewisman by birth, he came to work on the Brahan estate during the second half of the seventeenth century. He is credited with a great number of prophecies about the Highlands, especially the Inverness area. As well as these, like other seers he made various prophecies about the locally important family, the Mackenzies and their chiefs.

One such prediction was that the last of the line would be deaf and dumb, with four sons predeceasing him; while one of the daughters would kill her sister. Sure enough the male line was extinct by 1815, while in 1823 one sister died after being thrown from a carriage driven by her other sister. A monument at Brahan records the event to this day. Of another Mackenzie branch who lived at Fairbairn Tower, the seer predicted 'they shall disappear almost to a man from the face of the earth. Their castle shall become uninhabited and a cow shall give birth to a calf in

141

the top chamber of the tower.' Not only did the line end in 1851, but a cow wandered up the stone staircase in the following year, following a trail of hay which was by then stacked at the top of the deserted building. Sure enough, it then refused to descend and duly produced a calf, to the great wonderment of the town folk of Inverness. According to the local newspaper, the *Inverness Courier*, the locals visited the scene in large numbers.

In fact, the good folk of Inverness are very aware of their own seer, as the correspondence columns of the local paper frequently show. Many an Invernessian will earnestly explain how 'long lines of carriages without horses will run between Inverness and Dingwall and Skye', was a prediction on the coming of the railways; or that 'the days will come when fire and water shall run in streams through all the streets and lanes of Inverness' was a reference to the fact that in 1826 the Inverness Gas and Water Company opened for business, making Inverness one of the first towns in Scotland to have such supplies piped in.

Some of the prophecies attributed to the Brahan Seer are decidedly eerie. He said that when it was possible to cross the River Ness dry-shod in five places, a terrible disaster would strike the world. In 1939 Inverness had four bridges across the river, though one, a suspension bridge, had been condemned two years previously. The old suspension bridge was closed to vehicles but kept open for foot traffic until a temporary structure was built alongside. On completion of the temporary structure, the original was kept open for just a few days more, making five bridges in all. This happened in August 1939, just before Britain entered World War II.

The one prophecy most quoted and still feared in the Highlands is a complex one, already true in part, which sees the coming of the sheep and the new merchant proprietors, the emigration 'to islands now unknown' and finally the disturbing ending: 'after which the deer and other wild animals in the huge wilderness will be exterminated and browned by horrid black rains. The people will then return and take undisturbed possession of the lands of their ancestors.' Some point to nuclear fall-out from some terrible accident perhaps at Dounreay on the north coast, where the reactor plant may also become a storage site for other countries' nuclear waste. Others think this may be a reference to environmental catastrophe connected with North Sea oil or even the aftermath of some awful global holocaust.

As for the end of Brown Kenneth himself, traditional tales say that he had been summoned to entertain the guests of Lady Seaforth in the absence of her husband who was on the Continent (though why she wanted such gloomy entertainment is not recorded!). The seer was asked by Lady Seaforth during the evening what her husband was doing at that precise moment. With spectacular lack of tact he said that he saw her husband on his knees dallying (to say the least) with a young lady in Paris. For this accurate vision he was burned in a tar barrel at Chanonry Point near Fortrose. A plaque on a boulder recalls the unhappy event. However, this tradition is strongly contested as it seems likely Coinneach Odhar had become confused with another earlier 'Kenneth Owir', who had been

Opposite: The eastern shorelines of Scotland have plenty of rugged and unspoilt places, such as those around Tarbat Ness on the tip of the Black Isle. A number of mermaid tales are associated with this area – thus there is as good a chance of finding one here as anywhere else on Scotland's coastline.

143

accused of witchcraft about a century earlier and seems a much more likely candidate for the violent end so beloved of witchcraft trials at that time. In fact, it is possible that the later Brown Kenneth attracted other stories to him originally related by other seers, especially since contemporary documents relating to the Brahan Seer have not been traced. However, the Brahan Seer is only at the head of a great body of folk in the Highlands and elsewhere with the gift of second sight, or the ability to see visions, some of which relate to the future while others relate to the ghostly past.

The wee folk and their friends

Strange sights and visions take on many forms. People encounter things they cannot explain. There is, for example, a strong tradition of mermaids being seen along Scotland's coastlines.

Mermaids and fin folk

A man who lived in a village near the Bullers of Buchan, a great cauldron in the rocky sea coast south of Peterhead, was said to have conversed with a mermaid below the cliffs nearby, or so the local story goes. Another mermaid was apparently seen cavorting close to a local vessel just before it foundered on rocks along the same coastline. In *Scenes and Legends of the North of Scotland* (1860), Hugh Miller tells in detail the story of how a love-lorn shipmaster acquired the girl of his dreams only after seeing a mermaid near the town of Cromarty. He sneaked up on the unfortunate creature and grabbed her by the waist. He only let go after she had granted him three wishes, the last of which was to marry the local girl with whom he had fallen in love.

Mermaids thus had a part to play in the affairs of menfolk, who took advantage of their powers if they could. A boat builder at Gairloch early last century went to the rocky shore for bait. There he came across a mermaid asleep among the rocks. He grabbed her by the hair. The alarmed mermaid begged for release saying she would grant any boon which was asked. Clearly wishing to adopt an unbeatable marketing strategy, the boat builder made her promise that no one who sailed in any boat that he would ever make would be drowned.

In Orkney folklore, mermaids have a distinct pedigree, as the young daughters of the fin folk. The sea was home to the fin folk, who were hardly distinguishable from people on land except that they had supernatural powers. The fin man was dark and strong and had fins like a fish, though when on land he disguised them so that they seemed to be part of his clothing. The fin woman lost her beauty soon after marriage, according to tradition, and became ugly. Her one aim was to acquire silver money and she used her talent for curing diseases in both people and animals to

144

earn it. According to the old Orcadians, a mermaid could avoid her mother's fate of becoming ugly by marrying a human. She thus combed out her long golden hair and practised sweet singing as a way of attracting men. As for the inconvenience of her tail, this looked like a fine skirt when she was ashore, and in any case she lost this clue to her origins soon after marriage. Orcadian folklore warns that a man needed to be strong to resist the mermaids. Prayers, if said three times, could prove effective, but mermaids were dazzlingly radiant and could easily make men forget. This is why, until recent times among sea-going communities, any individuals who appeared uncannily clever at catching fish or predicting the weather would find themselves the victims of dark rumours about their grandfather being too familiar with a mermaid.

Sea trows and selkies

Another inhabitant of the sea around Orkney was the sea trow. In fact, the sea was full of them. Trow is, of course, similar to Scandinavian troll – a none-too-pleasant individual with the habit of capturing maidens and making them work for him. Sea trows were land trows who had been chased into the waters by their fellows. Like ordinary trows they were a bit stupid and lazy and thus had to make do with stealing fish off baited lines. Sometimes they came ashore as far as the beach but were frightened of the land trows.

From sea trows it is but a short swim to selkies. These are another denizen of Scotland's north and western waters, and are more usually known as Atlantic grey seals. (The common seals are sometimes called tangies or tang fish, while selkie is reserved for the less common and larger of the two species found in Scottish waters.) The main tradition centring around the selkie again concerns its dealing with man. Selkies, many of whom are half-human anyway, love to dance on the seashore, in human form, having cast aside their seal skin. In one commonly repeated tale a man walking by the shore finds a seal skin. Its owner, a beautiful seal woman, thus falls into his power. He marries her, they have several children and live happily for a time. One day, however, the seal woman finds the skin and puts it on, immediately vanishing to the sea, never to return.

Men also reveal themselves as half seal. The tale is told in the ballad 'The Grey Selkie of Suleskerrie':

> I am a man upon the land,
> I am a selchie in the sea,
> And when I'm far from every strand
> My dwellin is in Suleskerrie

Sule Skerry is an Atlantic rock about 50 miles south-west of Orkney, frequented by grey seals. In one version the song is sung by a mother lamenting to her child that she does not know where the bairn's father is. The father duly appears and offers her a purse of gold as a nurse's fee, though

145

his offer of marriage is refused. The mother places a gold chain on the neck of the child. Years later a gunner shoots a seal which is found to be wearing the chain, thus showing that the child has returned to the sea.

Other seal tales are of men being rescued by seals, or the recurring theme of a seal hunter being asked to accompany a stranger who suddenly appears at his hut by the seashore. The hunter is carried to a cliff and taken down below the sea to meet an injured selkie, surrounded by anxious relatives. The hunter is shown a knife, which it is claimed he lost while wounding the seal, which then swam off with the lodged knife. The stranger in the story, who is of course another selkie, explains that only the hunter can close the wound, after which he must swear an oath never to harm another seal. This the hunter does, so avoiding spending the rest of his life in the seal kingdom.

Some folklorists maintain that fin folk, selkies and trows are all closely related and possibly have a common origin. While Orkney, for example, is fairly specific in distinguishing between fins and seal folk (selkies), Shetland tends to group them together. However, stories about this class of creature – sea-going, half-human, partly fish or seal – are strongly centred on the Northern Isles and find their counterpart in Norwegian legends where they are called the huldrefolk, who are believed to have farms or kingdoms beneath the waves. One explanation for the origin of these curious tales lies in northern historians' accounts of strange men (and women) from a far northern country who occasionally turned up in Orkney and Shetland in kayaks (small craft covered in sealskin). These stories are not just from ancient tales – folklorists note references to a strange little man arriving in a kayak on the island of Eday in Orkney in 1862, and another on Westray two years later. There are similar reports from other islands in the eighteenth century plus an extraordinary record of a kayak voyager being found off Aberdeen, on the mainland, more than 100 miles to the south. (His kayak is in the Marischal College Museum.) A small individual, seemingly almost wrapped in sealskin and riding low in the water with a short paddle, seen over spray and wave-crests near a lonely shore, could look like a seal. Perhaps the seal-woman who lost her coat on the beach really lost the skin of her kayak. Thus she might have been some unfortunate far-northern Eskimo or, more likely, Lapplander blown off course like others of her race down the centuries. Fetching up in a strange community in the Northern Isles she was forced to stay, helping to reinforce legends of mysterious folk, small and round like seals, who had paddles for fingers.

Equally plausible, and possibly related, is the explanation that the fin folk were Lapps inhabiting the north of Scandinavia, who were taken as slaves by Norse settlers to Orkney and Shetland. As for the trows or trolls of these far north settlements, perhaps they were the original little inhabitants unable to cope with the superior technology of the Vikings. They took to frequenting wild and lonely places. Northern folk memory has recorded a few of their characteristics; sometimes they could be caught and set to work, sometimes they were seen as benevolent spirits, perhaps lurking around the edge of settlements hoping for food – tit-bits such as an occasional bowl of milk from the byre or a piece of bread.

Fairies

Back on land, there is also a very strong tradition of folklore associated with that wide-ranging genre of little folk, the fairies. In times gone by, they were easier to encounter. The Revd Robert Kirk (1644–92) was, for his time, an enlightened, earnest and humane minister who was appointed to Aberfoyle, southern gateway to the Trossachs, in 1685. Near the little Kirktoun of Aberfoyle can be seen Doon Hill, a rounded wooded hill, now with a marked nature trail winding up its side for the benefit of today's visitors. This little hill was to play an important part in the career of Aberfoyle's unusual minister. He was continually drawn to its slopes and spent hours each night with his ear pressed to the ground. Then he started work on a manuscript called 'The Secret Commonwealth of Elves, Fauns and Fairies'. The Doon Hill was a *dun sithean* (pronounced shee-an) or fairy hill. (The word for fairy in Gaelic, sometimes *bean-sith*, gives the English banshee, as well as numerous Scottish place names such as Glenshee and Schiehallion.)

Among the many facts recorded about the fairy folk in Kirk's work was that they adopted the dress of whatever part of the country they lived in, and that they could make themselves appear or disappear at will. He also related tales of other folk who, like Thomas the Rhymer, had been taken

Seat of the Clan Macleod, Dunvegan Castle on Skye is also the home of the Fairy Flag, a mysterious piece of cloth which tradition says can protect the clan in time of dire need.

away to Fairyland and returned in some time-warped way. The minister completed his treatise on the fairies in 1692 and shortly afterwards felt compelled to visit Doon Hill again one night. There he apparently suffered a fit, and was discovered dead, clad only in his nightshirt. However, the minister's remarkable story does not end with his death. After his funeral service, amid rumours that his body had disappeared and that his family had simply buried a weighted coffin, he reappeared before a relative. Kirk told him that he had been taken into Fairyland but could be returned to his own kind if, at the imminent baptism of Kirk's child, the local laird would throw an iron knife over his shoulder when Kirk appeared. (Fairy folk, according to Kirk's own treatise, were terrified of cold iron.) At the baptism held at the manse, Kirk materialised as he had predicted but the local laird was so astonished that he failed to act. With a reproachful look Kirk disappeared and according to tradition is trapped in Fairyland to this day. Meanwhile his manuscript, held by the minister's elder son, a respectable Edinburgh lawyer, later disappeared for a while but was rediscovered by Sir Walter Scott. Eventually it was printed in book form. Today's visitors wandering on the Doon Hill, guidebook in hand, may not be aware that Fairyland lies so close by – in caves in the hillsides, it is said. (On a personal note, I once walked round the hill in dead of winter and was surprised to note at one point a mysterious scent of curiously sweet perfume on the otherwise deserted track. Some descriptions of the Gaelic Tir-nan-Og, the land of eternal youth, speak of it being 'fanned by perfumed breezes'. Strangely, I also heard a chiffchaff singing that day in January. Normally this little warbler is only a summer visitor.)

Look into the history of any local Scottish parish and somewhere there is sure to be a reference to fairies. In the 1880s some boys reported that they saw fairies at the (appropriately named) Sitheanan Dubha at the north end of the Isle of Ewe, the sea loch on the north-western seaboard. The people on the mainland township of Mellon Charles, opposite the island, were not surprised as they often saw lights and heard music coming from offshore. Highland fairies were very musical and they often passed on their gifts to folk they met. There are a number of versions of this passing on of talent from fairies, often involving a herd boy on his own confronted by a fairy who gives him a chanter (the fingered part of the bagpipe). He then returns home to astonish his family by being able to play the pipes properly.

Another famous gift from the fairies, and one which is on view for all to see today, is the Fairy Flag of Dunvegan Castle on Skye. This tattered and yellowing piece of fabric, sealed behind glass, is the most treasured possession of the Clan Macleod. When analysed by modern scientific method the fabric was found to be silk from Rhodes or Syria and dating somewhere around the fourth to seventh centuries. However, such mundane considerations do not prevent many of the Clan Macleod believing that somehow it was given to an early Macleod chieftain by the fairies. There are various versions of how this came about. In one, the Lady of Macleod heard singing coming from the chamber in which her infant son slept. She

148

investigated and found a little woman in a green dress crooning over Macleod's child and smoothing over him a silken coverlet or banner. In another story a Macleod chief had taken a fairy for a wife and she had borne him a son, but almost immediately afterwards she pined for Fairyland and planned to return. The couple parted at the Fairy Bridge near Dunvegan, whereupon she gave him the banner. A further version has her parting at the bridge without the banner and the chief returning to Dunvegan Castle where a great celebration had been planned to honour the new baby. The nurse detailed to look after the child neglected him for a few moments in order to glimpse the feasting in the main hall below. The child meanwhile, disturbed by an owl, started to cry; he was heard by his mother in Fairyland, who then came and comforted him with the banner as a coverlet. This was discovered by the nurse, who brought the child in triumph into the hall, still covered by his new shawl, to the accompaniment of mysterious lullabies and fairy music.

In all versions the conditions for the keeping of the banner or Fairy Flag are the same: that it can be used to protect the clan three times only. Most versions of the tale say that it has been used twice in the past, at the Battle of Glendale in 1490 and at Waternish in 1580. Some say the second occasion the flag was unfurled was when a plague struck all of the Macleod cattle. However, yet another version in print unkindly suggests that the flag was unfurled and waved a third time by a sceptic called Buchanan in 1799. At the time, the flag was kept in a sealed iron chest and the treacherous Buchanan committed an even more dastardly act when he employed the village blacksmith to force open the casket. This version of the tale aside, some potency is still associated with Am Bratach Sith (Gaelic for the Fairy Banner). Even in World War II, RAF pilots from the clan carried a picture of the flag as a lucky charm. However, it would be misleading to select gift-giving as the only activity in which the fairies involve themselves.

Some say fairies represent a folk memory of a pygmy race driven into the woods and wild places by the arrival of new Celtic settlers. Others explain the notion by describing the fairies as native spirits who have somehow taken on human form. In any event, they are usually invisible to mortal eyes, except to those who have second sight. Artefacts such as the Fairy Flag are a symbol of the power of the fairies, which can still be acknowledged by believers.

Brownies and urisks

The fairies and their kin are only one among several kinds of nature spirits found in Scotland's wild places. Brownies and urisks could also at one time be found in plenty. While brownies were seen as helpful, harmless little souls, happy with the occasional offering of warm milk from the dairymaid, urisks were much more the outdoor independent type. They looked like the half-men, half-goat creatures that the Greeks called satyrs. Like deer they kept to the high tops in summer, but winter would drive them down to the glen. Sometimes they would hang about homesteads

and could be bribed into performing useful tasks, if the owner took care. In fact, the urisk responded to human kindness.

The Trossachs and Loch Lomond were favourite urisk haunts and Corrie Nan Uirisgean (sometimes translated as the goblins' cave, lair or corrie) is mentioned both in Scott's *The Lady of The Lake* and also on today's Ordnance Survey maps. The Clan Macfarlane had their headquarters near Loch Lomond and it is said that one of their chiefs had the wife of an urisk as his nurse and foster mother. On Speyside, the ancient family of Tullochgorun employed a pair of urisks, thought to be husband and wife. The wife in particular, known as Mag Mulloch or Hairy Meg, was very competent around the kitchen, but inclined to tell tales about the other servants' shortcomings to the mistress of the house. The servants probably thought that Hairy Meg was a 'clipe' and a 'big sook', which is what Scots call a tale teller and someone who deliberately courts favour.

Fairies take on all kinds of forms. In the Hebrides, a fairy with long flowing hair (of either sex) was known as a Gruagach. This fairy's job was to stop cattle falling over cliffs or stumbling into bogs. Like the brownie, a nightly offering of milk was expected. Brownies themselves were called Brunaidh in Gaelic, a word borrowed from Lowland Scots. The third kind of household fairy in Gaelic lore was the Glaistig. Her dress was green but her face was pale, hence the name (*glas* is Gaelic for grey). Her nightly job was to sweep and arrange the furniture, and particularly benevolent fairy staff of this kind could be persuaded to spin as well.

A phantom array

Some still may claim to hear or see fairies and their friends from time to time. But not all the flitting visions in quiet places in Scotland are necessarily the wee folk. Scotland is a favourite haunting country for ghosts. Phantom pipers, ghostly coachmen, Roman soldiers, a grey dog or two, marching armies which suddenly disappear, a ghostly airman, a Highlander on the Culloden battlefield, an old woman evicted during the Clearances, ghostly monks forever doomed to re-enact their slaughter by raiding Vikings. Indeed, the Scottish experience is incomplete without its ghostly encounters. The empty Highlands, with their dark woods, wild glens and ruined castles, certainly have a large share of things seen but unexplained. However, the Lowlands, including the Borders and cities, also have their chilling tales. The apparition of a headless workman wearing dungarees and boots was seen several times in 1968 at the Ravenscraig Steelworks in Motherwell, usually in the vicinity of the Number Two blast furnace. In 1962, the A75 between Dumfries and Annan near the Solway Firth was haunted by, of all things, a phantom furniture van which on more than one occasion almost caused an accident when suddenly encountered by other motorists at night. Even the romantic Isle of Skye

manages a motorised ghost: a 1934 Austin which runs silently but at breakneck speed on the road near Sligachan. In fact, from such bizarre apparitions it seems almost a relief to turn to more conventional ghosts.

Traditionally, all the best castles are steeped in legend. Of these, Glamis Castle in Angus, the ancient seat of the Lyon Family, is famous. Probably the earliest legend tells how the fairy folk interfered with the building of the castle. 'Fiery Pans' or the summit of Hunter's Hill was the intended site. Builders set to work, but whatever progress was made was rudely retarded by night. Eventually a voice was heard proclaiming: 'Build the castle in a bog where 'twill neither shak nor shog.' So the castle was built in the lush Vale of Strathmore where it has stood for 600 years. The secret chamber has given rise to many a legend. The room is thought to be on the north-facing wall of the crypt, and a blocked up window can be seen from the outside. The favourite tale is of Lord Glamis and his old enemy the Tiger Earl of Crawford, who gambled with dice late on a Saturday night. An old retainer reminded them of the lateness of the hour and that it was nearly the sabbath. At five minutes to midnight he returned and pointed to the time. 'I care not what day of the week it is', roared Lord Glamis. 'If we have a mind to we shall play on until Doomsday.' They played on and as the last note of midnight chimed, the door opened and a cold breeze blew in. In the doorway stood a tall, slim man dressed in black. 'I will take your Lordship at your word', he intoned. 'Doomsday has come for you.' The story is that they sit there playing still.

The island of Iona off the west coast of Mull is often described as the cradle of Scottish Christianity. It seems to affect visitors in different ways. Some find it peaceful, its beaches and flowery grazings the very essence of west-coast charm and tranquillity. However, others find it unsettling.

Iona was certainly the scene of dreadful bloodshed. The pious monks of the Abbey were often attacked by pagan Viking raiding parties when unspeakable atrocities were committed. Since that time many have reported visions of monks in their simple brown robes and other such hauntings; but on one particular moonlit night a member of the Iona Community (a modern religious body active within the restored Abbey) had an even more dramatic experience. On his way to visit a friend on a croft, not only did he fail to find the building, but also lost all other island landmarks of modern times. He approached the White Sands, one of the island's many dazzling little beaches, and suddenly a fleet of Viking craft appeared offshore, bearing down on the beach where a group of monks stood. The ships disembarked a party of fierce well-armed warriors who cut down the monks before making their way towards the Abbey. Soon they returned bearing booty and driving cattle. The vision then faded – to be added to the store of ghostly tales told about this enchanted isle, where, some say, past and present can become entangled.

Most people would accept that all places have 'atmosphere', which can make us feel anything from tranquil to highly uneasy. Scotland can certainly feel 'spooky', even when the visitor least expects it. A quiet evening's walk among the tall pines of Speyside can be made slightly unsettling

by an unexpected and ghostly coughing bark somewhere close by – a curious sound whose direction is difficult to trace. The light is dimming – is there movement in the juniper thicket? Probably yes, because grazing roe deer make strange noises and become active at dusk. Even the sight of the deer bounding through the trees in the half-light may cause a momentary shiver. Tales of ghostly animals come to mind, but the imagination can be strangely stimulated in wild and beautiful landscapes.

Little wonder then that the area around Speyside and the Cairngorms has its share of creepy tales. The high domes of the Cairngorms are lonely places. When the mist drifts down, the very stones take on the shape of half-seen figures. Perhaps the most famous Cairngorm ghost is the Big Grey Man of Ben Macdhui (Am Fear Liath Mor), a modern-day giant no less, said to haunt the hills. He made his most lasting impression in 1891 on Professor Norman Collie, a sober and distinguished scientist and member of the Royal Society. While walking in mist across the broad summit of 1,309 m (4,296 ft) high Ben Macdhui, the learned gentleman was surprised to hear footsteps behind him, from something which sounded as though it was taking one step for every three or four which he took. His own account of this odd sensation as printed in the *Cairngorm Club Journal*, Vol. XI, no. 64 (June 1926), is vivid:

> I said to myself, 'This is all nonsense.' I listened and heard it again but could see nothing in the mist. As I walked on and the eerie crunch, crunch, sounded behind me I was seized with terror and took to my heels, staggering blindly among the boulders for four or five miles nearly down to Rothiemurchus Forest.
>
> Whatever you make of it I do not know, but there is something very queer about the top of Ben Macdhui and I will not go back there again by myself I know.

The climbing fraternity are usually great story-tellers and soon there were other stories of a presence with crunching footsteps. One naturalist who encountered a looming shape in the mist near the summit plateau was actually armed (it was 1943) and fired his revolver at 'the thing'. One tale recounts how an experienced Everest mountaineer, while on the Ben one clear June night in the early years of the century, saw a figure climb out of the Lairig Ghru, the pass below, and walk round the summit cairn before disappearing. The mountaineer was 'struck dumb' by the sheer size of the figure – apparently the same height as the cairn, which he reckoned to be about 3 m (10 ft) high. This all sounds very dramatic but the summit plateau is featureless, especially in mist where size and distance are hard to judge. It could have been another climber; perhaps it was a classic case of expecting to see something eerie and unconsciously adjusting the facts to fit. Nevertheless, the tales of crunching footsteps or malign presences were persistent and began to spread. In the early years of the century, travellers occasionally encountered an uncanny spirit amongst the Speyside pinewoods, particularly around Rothiemurchus. In 1929 there was even correspondence about it in *The Times* of London.

Today, however, chair-lifts and ski developments have opened up access to the plateau, and the explosion of outdoor activities has made the Cairngorms seem much less remote.

The mountain mists of Speyside can prey on the minds of the imaginative, especially after a long day getting to the top of Ben Macdhui, but even the gentle banks of the River Spey at lower levels can be the backdrop for odd happenings. A spot a little way downstream from the bridge at Boat of Garten was the setting, not for a ghostly encounter, but for a bizarre incident which, though documented, does not fit easily into any category, except that of a miracle.

According to the story, in the 1860s there was an old woman living at Tulloch, near Loch Garten, south of the river, who wished on her death to be buried in the Duthil churchyard across the broad River Spey to the north. Her relatives pointed out that this might not be possible, especially if the river was high. However, the woman specified a place where, she assured them, her cortège would cross in safety when the appropriate day came. In due course she died and on the day of her funeral the river was in flood. Nevertheless the funeral party made its way to the spot as instructed. Suddenly the waters of the river parted and the procession was able to cross dry-shod. The waters immediately closed again and flowed on as usual. This dramatic event unsettled many local folk and though a memorial stone was erected in 1865 to record the miracle, the more strait-laced church sects condemned the whole proceedings as an abomination.

Even stranger, the tale does not end there. Two years later, the memorial was found broken and thrown into the river. The largest piece was later retrieved by a farmer, who then used it as a doorstep. From that day his house was haunted, until finally he was forced to return the stone to the river. Years later, some local boys tampered with fragments of the broken memorial which they found when the water was low. One by one the boys died for various reasons soon afterwards – a warning to folk not to tamper with the inscribed chunks of what has become known as the Stone of Spey.

Canine spectres

Not all of Scotland's ghosts have human forms: there are several canine spectres. A grey dog is said to haunt the road around Arisaig on the popular Fort William to Mallaig route. The story goes that it was left behind by its owner during the notorious Clearances, when many families took sail for Nova Scotia, and that it was abandoned to search forever for its vanished master. At least, that is one explanation. Another is that the dog is an omen of death, which evolved from an incident when a Macdonald of Morar, owner of a very large greyhound about to litter, left home to fight in a foreign war. When he returned home the pups had grown huge. They attacked and killed Macdonald as he entered his own home, before the dogs' mother could intervene.

Even amid the bustle of Glasgow, Scotland's largest city, there is said to

Many Highland lochs are associated with tales of strange monsters. Loch Chon, near Aberfoyle in the beautiful Trossachs, is just one of them. This is the home, according to tradition, of a strange dog-headed monster with the unpleasant habit of eating unwary passers-by.

be a canine ghost inhabiting a house in Duke Street, just a few minutes east of the city centre. A solicitor, who rented the property with his family, was alarmed when the children's nursemaid reported to him that his children were playing with something that looked like a dog. The solicitor investigated and saw a dog in blurred outline, coming from the nursery. The children, though quite undisturbed, were puzzled by the furry animal which they could never touch. After other odd encounters the family moved out and the case was investigated by a researcher into paranormal happenings. While spending an evening in the darkened house he was called upon by a policeman, who was suspicious of lights moving in the otherwise deserted property. As the researcher explained to the policeman that he was investigating a ghost, the officer pointed upstairs and commented that he certainly would not be frightened with an animal like that for company. The researcher turned to see a large dog backing off and apparently disappearing into the wall half-way up the stairs. Both men hurriedly left the house and did not return!

154

A Gaelic bestiary

Perhaps the Cu-sith or fairy dog was part of an old Gaelic belief which migrated with the Gaels from the country to the city. To hear its bark apparently meant certain death to the hearer. Some say the Cu-sith was very large – perhaps the size of a small cow – and had enormous feet. It was particularly associated with Benbecula in the Outer Isles. But Loch Chon, west of Aberfoyle in the Trossachs, has a tale about a dog-headed monster which was said to be partial to passers-by. Perhaps it, too, was a Cu-sith. Meanwhile, hardly a year goes by without someone, somewhere spotting some kind of mysterious large cat, often in the Highlands.

Likewise other domestic animals take their place in this mythical Gaelic bestiary. In Martin Martin's *A Description of the Western Islands of Scotland*, there is reference to Crodh-mara, or sea cows, which were said to be like ordinary cattle but for the most part lived in the sea, though sometimes they came ashore and mingled with other cattle. Not that this belief in mysterious water-borne cattle was confined to the Highlands. James Hogg, friend of Scott and fellow writer, and known as the Ettrick Shepherd, was steeped in the lore of the Scottish Borders. He relates how a water cow frequented St Mary's Loch in the heart of the Border country. A local farmer secured one of her offspring and in due course, thanks to the exceptional fertility of the animal, his herd greatly increased. However, things went wrong for the farmer after he somehow offended the original watery parent. She gave a great roar, whereupon all her descendants left the pastures, trooped off into the loch and were never seen again!

Naturally, where there are water cows, tradition also finds a place for *tarbh-uisge* (Gaelic, meaning water bull). According to legend, these frequented lochs and rivers in many parts of Scotland, particularly out-of-the-way hill lochs. Dr Macculloch, a traveller in 1824 who later published his narrative in London, relates how he came across a farmer busy with his two sons by the side of a loch. The farmer had a gun and the two sons were agitating the surface of the water, apparently in an attempt to dislodge an unusually predatory water bull which had been rampaging around, disturbing the farmer's flocks. The farmer's gun was loaded with sixpences because, as he informed the traveller, the creatures could only be destroyed by silver bullets. Another troublesome *tarbh-uisge* once frequented Kirkmichael, on the way to Glenshee in Perthshire. This one charged around the banks, making life difficult for local anglers. Accounts of its appearance vary, with some saying it was black yet soft and velvety.

The most famous mythical beast of all is the water horse, or *each-uisge* in Gaelic. This is also, on occasion, called the kelpie, but there seems to be a running together of two kinds of traditions, one involving kelpies who seemed to frequent burns and other Highland torrents and an equally notorious collection of loch monsters whose presence is indicated in the Highlands by a number of lochs called Loch na Beiste or the loch of the

155

beast. While most folk today would consign the kelpie to the realms of imagination, the traditional loch monster refuses to go away. The kelpie of folklore preferred deep pools, rivers and burns. Usually he took the form of a black horse. His speciality was approaching weary foot travellers, or alternatively innocent bands of children, and by some means persuading them to mount. The kelpie would then plunge into his home pool and drown the victim. Just one story from many is set in beautiful Balquhidder Glen, north of Callander. Tradition tells of a horse (milk white, by way of variety) which approached some children playing by the loch. By its docility and friendliness it enticed all the children on its back before it took its fatal plunge.

However, the kelpie could be used to carry out heavy work if he was caught. This was made easier by the fact that he tended to frequent farmstead sheilings, a habit which he seemed to share with most other mythical beasties. If an opportunity presented itself a bridle on which the sign of the cross had been made was thrown over the kelpie's head. Then he became docile and could be used around the homestead.

Other Highland traditions say that the kelpie's own bridle had special properties. If by any chance a kelpie's bridle was found, apparently by looking through the eyelets of the bridle bit, the spirit kingdom with all its to-ing and fro-ing of fairies would become visible. The possessor of such a device was then able to work much white magic, curing and healing, and probably earning a high reputation for miles around.

Lochs with water horse associations include Loch Treig in Lochaber, so if you are lucky enough ever to travel on the beautiful West Highland railway line, keep a sharp lookout; also Loch Lomond, Loch Shiel in the western Highlands, Loch Morar and, most famous of all, Loch Ness. The mystery of 'Nessie', in particular, has captured the imagination of people across the world. However, a good 80 years before the Loch Ness monster first courted publicity in a tantalising way in the 1930s, at least one other monster caused ripples. The setting was on the headland of Rubha Mor, between Loch Ewe and Gruinard Bay in Wester Ross.

The usual route of a small company of churchgoers travelling homewards to the settlement of Mellon Udrigle, took them past a loch about 549 m (600 yds) long. On one occasion they suddenly saw, rising from the peaty waters, a dark shape like an upturned boat keel. It sank below the surface almost immediately. The story got around and a short while later was corroborated when the phenomenon was spotted again by another reliable and sober witness. The local population, perhaps of superstitious inclination, were much disturbed by the idea that a kelpie or monster of some kind was lurking in the depths of their local loch. They looked for help from the local laird, a rich industrialist Englishman called Bankes. Hoping to appear as a benevolent proprietor Bankes decided to act to get rid of the beast, and set his mind upon draining the loch. First, drainage channels were dug, then a hand pump was set up. Unfortunately, after two years' work the water level of the loch had been reduced by only a few inches! In this time the locals had continued to be uneasy and Bankes had

become a laughing stock for his unsuccessful project. To save face he procured 14 barrels of lime and had them dumped in the loch to make the loch uninhabitable. By coincidence the goings-on at this loch, Loch Na Beiste – which, incidentally, was given its name long before the 1850s when Bankes was active here – took place towards the end of a minor phase of sea-monster sightings which kept many newspapers busy. (The press using a good monster story is no twentieth-century phenomenon.) The magazine *Punch* got hold of the Loch Na Beiste story and published a piece in which the activity of the English landlord was ridiculed. He retaliated by raising his tenants' rents in an attempt to recoup his expenses. At least the beast was never seen again, even refusing to put in an appearance during the next bout of monster mania, during which 'Nessie' was born.

The Loch Ness monster

The Loch Ness monster is a phenomenon of tradition, folklore – and modern publicity. In fact it could be said that it represents Scottish tradition in its most marketable form. The Scottish Tourist Board has statistics which show that the Loch Ness monster is one of the first enquiries made by the Japanese when they arrive in Scotland, knowing very few other facts about the country. The phenomenon sustains at least two visitor centres, in addition to the accommodation and catering industry around the loch. Souvenirs and books on the subject are available in plenty.

The story started around 1930 when the local *Northern Chronicle* published an item about anglers disturbed by a commotion in the waters of Loch Ness. The newspaper requested comment and received several letters describing other strange incidents. The *Inverness Courier* took up the story in 1933 and published another sighting report. This in turn sparked off other newspapers to investigate, and soon the phenomenon was big news. The *Daily Mail* even employed a game hunter to track down the beast; while, at the same time, the first of the practical jokers entered the arena, leaving spectacular clues in the form of impressions on a sandy stretch of the Loch Ness shoreline, using the mounted foot of a hippopotamus!

One of the most famous monster portraits was taken in April 1934 and showed the classic head and neck pose. The photographer, Mr A. K. Wilson based in London, claimed only to have photographed an object moving in Loch Ness. Perhaps it was the monster, or possibly the tail of a diving otter.

After the war, interest continued unabated. Rocks in the shallows, boats' wakes crossing in still water, swimming red deer, diving cormorants and many more natural events, have all caused hearts to beat faster for a moment. By the 1960s matters were getting really serious. Cameras and searchlights were tried, while underwater listening devices, infra-red night cameras, sonar scanners and submarines were all employed at one time or another. By the mid 1970s a few tantalising shapes had been recorded by means of underwater cameras.

A sober assessment might conclude that there was something odd going on. The appearance of the monster was in inverse proportion to the number of cameras and other devices which were working in the loch at any one time. Nessie, it seemed, specialised in near misses, *almost* appearing on film quite a lot. However, at least those investigating were finding out a great deal about the loch and its many inhabitants. This great trench along a major fault line goes down to over 244 m (800 ft). Trawling at great depth revealed a possible food source: tiny mussels, copepods, worms and midge larvae. (This last species confirmed a horrid vision in Scots' minds: that if midges can survive on the bed of Loch Ness, then they are truly inescapable in Scotland.) Sonar scans in the early 1980s also revealed large 'targets' moving in the water which could not easily be explained as shoals of fish. As ever, the evidence remained tantalisingly unconvincing. Believers claim that hundreds of witnesses have seen something so out of the ordinary that in some cases it has even changed their lives. They see the lack of photographic proof as evidence of the creature's intelligence – it simply shuns the limelight. The family of monsters – because there must be several – have by now become adept at keeping out of the way. The sceptics point out that Loch Ness is a very large body of water that can have distorting effects on local weather. Snow seldom lies long on its banks, and the warming influence of the loch is more pronounced on still days when it can even give rise to local mirage conditions. Rocks in the shallows, or swimming water birds, can be magnified and elongated in the shimmering air to produce the strangest optical effects.

Whatever the truth of the matter, Scotland needs its water horse. In the modern commercial world, it is a wonderful tourist attraction and, for that reason alone, it is in no one's interest for the matter to be resolved. But in an emotional sense it is also relevant. The phenomenon belongs to an earlier age when the imagination was more important; when belief in fairies or mermaids or kelpies was part of the fabric of the folk culture. The Loch Ness Monster and its cousins, perhaps still lurking in other lochs in the Highlands, allow us to stay in touch with the traditions of earlier times. Perhaps, Scots and non-Scots alike, we need our monsters – as a reminder that not quite everything has been controlled and explained in an increasingly technological and material world.

INDEX

Page numbers in *italics* refer to illustrations and their captions